NORMANDY

TEXT
PHILIPPE BERTIN

PHOTOGRAPHS
PIERRE BERENGER

TRANSLATION:ENTREPRISES 35

Éditions Ouest-France

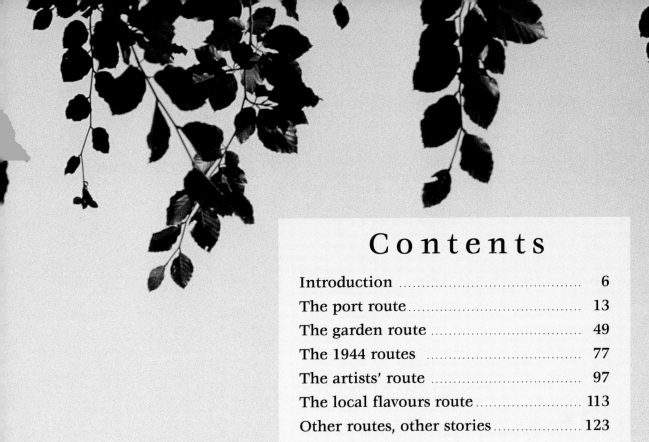

Contents

THE PATH IS ROUGH, a very narrow alley between two old buildings, corroded by the sand. The spot itself is beautiful, often completely silent. In the old days, a few fishermen lived here, at the foot of the rocks, in the shadow of the fort which feels the swell and treasure in the deepest depths of the jungle. Never tire of these moments. Never forget that here, at land's end, in a forgotten corner of the Cotentin, the evenings are blessed by the Gods. The light is soft and beautiful. A water-colour: a master's painting; a little marvel.

Wandering along,

defends la Hougue. The site is not to be found on the tourist maps, it is only known by a few regulars who come here to watch the night falling over the bay.

In summer, with the first warm days, a few houses around echo with the cries of children off to conquer the strands just as others searched for

Opposite, on the other coast of the peninsula, the winds are wilder. When the storm approaches, they can even be heard groaning inside the heavy stones of the houses. The trees bend their backs from so much wind. In the mist, their branches make strange shapes at the feet of the old stone walls: this is a bit of Ireland, a land engorged with

On the shores of the Val de Saire, in the Cotentin: the Hougue fort.

The Hague landscape, Escalgrain bay: trees bent by the winds and weather.

the paths of Normandy...

water, heaths which plunge into the sea and form this country, which they say here is like an island.

On the coast, the customs officers' footpath is a reminder of old stories: pirates' country, these "brigands" arriving by sea from neighbouring isles, from Alderney or Guernsey, to face the Blanchard race like the old pirates on the high seas. Tales tell that, once on the shore, they managed to foil the "gabelous", or salt-tax collectors, the ancestors of our customs officers. This countryside is a real treasure. As Jean-François Millet wrote "Suddenly one comes across a wide sea view and a limitless horizon". At the foot of the old house he lived in, in the hamlet of Gruchy at Gréville-Hague, the old well is still intact: a witness of former times, stone worn by the wind and hail which tells us about the happiness of being there in those days, chalking the close-by landscapes, the old and rugged cliffs blackened by big clouds above the waves as the sun set.

Further south, follow the small path which leads from the foot of Mont Castel and climbs up the cliff. This is the favourite walk for lovers on Sundays: they climb above Port-en-Bessin, a pretty fishing port "opening" onto the sea, and adventure along the pastures which overlook the open sea. The view is breathtaking from here: all at once,

Port-en-Bessin:
a pretty creek in the sea.

Marshes of the Veys bay: an amazing view.
(Photo André Mauxion, from "The Wild Manche ", Ouest-France publications, 2000)

Behind the dunes, in the swampy region, Normandy is a paradise for nesting birds – curlew-sandpipers shown here.
(Photo André Mauxion, from "The Wild Manche", Ouest-France publications, 2000)

when the sky is clear and fine, the long beaches which mark the history of the country can be seen at a glance.

To the north, the coast leads to the port of the bay of Les Veys. Still further, Utah Beach, beaches of fine sand protected by narrow lines of dunes. To the south, the remains of an artificial port known throughout the world, Arromanches, before Hoc Point.

Behind the liberation beaches, the countryside is organised around water springs and marshes which, when the first winter rains arrive, are swollen by the rivers to the point of transforming them into lakes. Barbey d'Aurevilly, child of Saint-Saveur-le-Vicomte, in the département of the Manche, recounts how it was an adventure in days gone by to cross the marshes marking this peninsula. There is the sound of the sea, and the sound of the wind rushing between two sand hills. In spring there is the murmur of the streams crossing the pastures at the foot of pretty manors. This is a gentle country, with an angel's skin, a little treasure.

The beaches, the sand, wandering southwards along the eastern coast, gave birth fairly recently to the fashion of sea-water baths and smart spas. The old dwellings are wealthy, and some of them have become famous because of their history, the source of inspiration for writers. In Cabourg, the promenade is named after one of the most famous. Is the Marcel Proust room in the Grand Hotel today the same as that known by the author of such fine pages? It does not really matter since the memory and the scents of a blessed time remain, a little antiquated.

Here, the coast can tell of worldly evenings, meetings and unfaithful loves. Deauville, Trouville, Houlgate, the black rocks, the cliff, the walks on the broad walk or behind the dunes, the Hermanville front, the narrow streets of Sainte-Adresse, the big bourgeois houses with their heavy stone and fine cornices: here, more than elsewhere, one needs to take one's time, and the side roads, to find out behind the postcards what is the real charm of a land which never takes any wrinkles, is never effaced.

Behind this special world, there is another. Quite different, just as astonishing. Old lost manors, beautiful villages between two river banks, secret gardens hidden by high walls and protected from indiscreet glances. This is the land of painters, writers, men and women who watch the sky and its light to extract the essential, intimate secrets. Sometimes it is said that peaceful paths can lead to the most beautiful of kingdoms. That it takes nothing, or almost nothing, to understand the soul of a country. It is enough to lose your way, under the trees, along a river, to listen to the winds singing and to breathe deeply, to detect the perfume of grasses which have hardly faded. It is said that it takes only a little effort to discover the unbelievable, the most astonishing of paths.

Look at this Normandy, this land's end, these rugged and sheer cliffs, these soft hills and these stones from another age. See how pleasing it is to push open the door of a little house with hidden secrets, and to find inside

the soul of the poet, or still to be able to feel the fever of the colours dashed on the canvas to create a treasure. Notice, at dawn, the mist lifting from over the pastures numbed in a deep sleep which has not yet been disturb-

*The house where
Sarah Bernhardt lived in
Sainte-Adresse (Seine-Maritime).*

*Half-timbered houses:
the " landscape" of
traditional Normandy.*

ed. This is a little marvel, a land which resembles no other: it is the history of those who left, like gentle dreamers, to conquer forbidden kingdoms. It bears the mark of incredible battles and terrible suffering. It is the sign of rediscovered freedom, hope which was never extinguished.

This is the land to be discovered by following the paths which contribute to understanding it better. The route leads along the coast to the most beautiful creeks, the finest beaches, tiny and wild ports, dreamlike places with a beauty which is almost simple. The route leads to small villages set in the

Normandy costumes at the
beginning of the 20th century.
(Monique Sclaresky collection)

countryside, old walls which time has not changed. The route leads to pretty châteaux, relics of a world which no longer exists, but is still present here. The route leads to many gardens, small corners of a cared-for, protected and adored universe. The route leads to so many sites, so many places, so many secrets that

North of the river Seine, the Alabaster Coast.

the travel guides should be forgotten, and the journey left to the wind and fortune.

We have decided to describe this Normandy, Lower and Upper Normandy, with chalk cliffs and steep rocks, dunes and deep countryside, freezing marshes and secret gardens, artists' houses and forgotten manors, woodland and pastures with centuries-old trees and ageing villages. We have chosen several stretches of land, making a strange and curious mosaic. Philippe Delerm, "the little sip of beer", has this fine formula to describe the Normandy he loves: "The paths invent us. And here are a few of them, the portrait of a region which changes as we go along, shows the contours of its rich history, talks to the heart of those who take the time, all their time, to love it even more. Wanderers, here are these routes of discovery.

Routes and discoveries: two perfect words to describe Normandy. They were made for this land...

The port route

Sheltered by the Hague

Let's begin with the smallest. Some will say that this is obvious – so many guides mention it – Port-Racine, a tiny shelter hidden from the winds by the Hague cape, tucked in between Omonville-la-Petite and Saint-Germain-des-Vaux, the land of Prévert and Jean-François Millet. Can we be certain?

Further south and further east, the Val de Saire, just next to the landing beaches, protects another. It is marked on the maritime charts for passing ships: in bygone days, in this very spot, sailors in quarantine were moored here. A long time ago, one of the biggest battles of all times between sailing ships took place here. The little port of Tatihou, a little confetti tossed by the waves; is it the smallest in France? Specialists and great connoisseurs of our maritime heritage must surely have their ideas on this question.

Does it really matter if Port-Racine and Tatihou are rivals over a few inches of jetty? Does it really matter if one or the other no longer receives many visitors? Both are places to arouse dreams of incredible voyages, and extraordinary epochs.

The other shore after Port-Racine is America. It is easy to imagine the liners which crossed the open seas, taking on men twenty years old at Cherbourg, visionaries or conquering emigrants. Imagine their first impression, the first dreams of men who left the Old World to find another. Astonishing travellers to the end of the earth: is this little port in the Manche among the last images which they carried with them when they left for the unknown, in quest of happiness and adventure?

Tiny port, a pin-head on the sea chart of absolute dreams; you saw rusty carcasses leave, newly painted and forging the waves, promising better days to come. Further off, and later, you also saw heavy

Opposite:
Goury, in the Contentin.
The very end of "land's end".

Port-Racine: the smallest port in France, in Cotentin.

Map legend:
★ Interesting port
♨ Lighthouse
▣ Religious building
🏰 Château

0 ———— 30 km

cargoes crossing, passing, coming and going, through the surf and making headway. At Port-Racine, take the road following the coast, which winds around the feet of the rocks, and see the frail boats moored at the quay, linked to the sea wall by ropes. Will these leave one day for other far-off places? Believe it, no. The images are always the same, summer and winter, spring and autumn: boats, the fishermen's dories, bits of wood set on the billows, are the long-time guests of a somnolent port. This port which protects them was born under Napoleon. It owes its name to that of a privateer who was looking for a calm haven sheltered from storms and inquisitive regards.

The Goury lighthouse. The most beautiful and most rugged part of the Hague.

This is an oddment, an exception, a little corner of sea and rock. It is also an attractive walk. All around Port-Racine, carved out of the Verte Roque, the nearby Hague rock offers all its best, the purest, the most rugged. It is not surprising that just a little way away some, like Trauner the cinema designer, or Prévert, the poet, found refuge here. The countryside, the sea, the horizon often masked by mist: the views are not banal here. Some say that the surroundings are too rugged for wandering peacefully. Others only want to come back again after their first discovery. As Didier Decoin says: "Living here, right next to Port-Racine, means accepting life with the people of the winds."

At Hague Cape, watch the sea swell, the billows boom. Feel the surge beating the sides of the old Goury lighthouse, at sea off Auderville: a gust of wind, and a storm is coming, an adventure beginning.

From Saint-Germain-des-Vaux or Omonville-la-Rogue, walks around the foot of the rocks give the impression of travelling far. Close to Port-Racine, do not miss the Prévert Garden, inspired by the neighbouring poet whose tombstone at Omonville-la Petite, looked after by Nénette, his former maid, looks over the sea. There are also the outlines of the Hague, from Port-Racine to Jobourg, from Saint-Germain to Goury, to be seen. The creeks, the rocks, the rough sand, and the stones to be found further away at low tide, are refuges for birds, also travellers. Other ports, other lifestyles: at Goury, sailors take refuge from the storms: the building of the Lifeguard

On the rocky sides of the "Jobourg Nose" a couple of crested cormorants.
(Photo André Mauxion, from "The Wild Manche", Ouest-France publications, 2000)

Around Port-Racine, the winds have wings: they carry the clouds which pass by, retell the legends and old stories about the "haguards", the local people, peasants, fishermen, and poets.

Society boat which is ready to set off when the worst happens, and in any weather, is next to the lighthouse warning of danger.

It is said that this is one of the most dangerous passages along the coast:

Tatihou, confetti tossed by the waves.

Gannet.
(Photo André Mauxion, from "The Wild Manche", Ouest-France publications, 2000)

The west coast of Cotentin, at the foot of Vauville.

peace, another way of looking at the sea: behind, the priory, the botanical garden and the bird reserve show that, when sheltered from the wind, everything becomes silent, even too calm. Little Port-Racine, an unavoidable part of the surroundings, little port of so many love-affairs, it is only those who never look at your neighbours who find you so small...

Barneville-Carteret: the memory of Mère Denis

On the west coast, take a look at Barneville-Carteret: it is impossible to describe the attraction of this rocky point and dunes. Barneville and Carteret, two associated communes, their finger pointed towards the Channel Islands opposite. Carteret Cape, above the port, offers an unparalleled panorama. At its feet, one of

the Blanchard race is a wall of water and currents, a ceaseless wave in motion.

On the coast the Vauville dunes, just next door but further south, seem almost gentle and restful in comparison. This is a haven of

Unloading:
a real event.

the most beautiful beaches of the west coast; 5 miles of fine sand right up to the Rozel Cape to the north. Nearby, the Hatainville dunes repre-

season. The resort was really born between the two World Wars, but there are traces dating it back to about 1840. Jules Barbey d'Aurevilly,

The beach "cabins"
at Barneville Carteret,
at the foot of the cape.

sent an exceptional natural heritage. Any walk here is always delightful. It leads you from the old wash-house of the famous Mère Denis (old French advertisement for washing powder), who came from around here.

There was a time when a steam-boat ensured the link with Jersey, in

native of Saint-Sauveur-le-Vicomte, came here on holiday from 1823, and they "remember" that in 1842, twenty-three people bathed in the sea for the first time! These days, the coast has a new life with its new yacht harbour – the Islands port – with its faithful visitors, including many English.

Saint-Vaast-la-Hougue:
Tatihou port.
(Monique Sclaresky collection)

The amphibious boat linking
Tatihou to
Saint-Vaast-la-Hougue.

Tatihou

A small port for such a long voyage: Tatihou belongs to the race of sea-farers from another age. The amphibious boat leaving from Saint-Vaast, takes us past the strands, and between the oyster beds. At low tide, there is such a din, such jostling, that the crossing is already something to remember. The port of Saint-Vaast, its rows of English boats, the old riggings preserved like antiques, its fishing boats which bring back their catch every week, is already far away. The outlines of the coast can be seen, to the north, Janville Point, a wonder of wonders, the customs officers' path which marks the way around the rock and then this small stone wall which wishes you welcome.

Easy to say: this island is a treasure island. Close to the mainland and yet so far from the world. To begin with the port: a minute gash which only lets little boats through, like dories. "The Ami Pierre", a fishing smack rebuilt in situ in the shipyards of Tatihou from old plans found and dating back to 1860, has its habits. When the weather is good, it goes out and takes young sea-goers ready to cross swords with the privateers.

Tatihou is everything, but where is Tatihou? A rare pearl, unique evidence of a revalued and renewed heritage, the site serves as an

example: it was saved from the waters by the Coastline Conservation Trust and the *Département* of the Manche, and has now become one of the figureheads of tourist policy for this coast. Things have happened since the renovation in 1992 and the underwater exploration campaign accompanying this rehabilitation work. Formerly, that is to say in recent times, the rock which was a "re-education centre" for young people in trouble, went through a

tumultuous history worthy of a real novel. It was the scene of numerous conquests and the famous battle of the Hougue in 1692, during which the Anglo-Dutch coalition obliterated the French navy. Tatihou was in turn a leper colony – the plague epidemic forced it to be so – a natural history museum – the adventure of aquaculture began here - a military prison during the First World War and, finally, a "holiday camp" before it was pillaged and neglected for much too long, nearly a decade.

The work to re-conquer the island bore its fruits: the Vauban tower, the former leper colony in the intra-muros part, the laboratory class-rooms, the square fort of the Ilet (tiny island) and several buildings recovered their smiles and new occupants. Nesting birds from the other side of the strand and pastures infested by rabbits, children taking courses by the sea in the canteen and the "dormitories", research botanists in the garden of rare herbs, those interested in local history, people looking for

shellfish and ordinary walkers: all this little world lives in perfect harmony respecting this site which does not allow in more tourists than it can deal with. Be careful; better not drop your rubbish on the rocks if you do not want to be shouted at loudly by Eugène, the guardian who keeps an eye on everything.

Tatihou is busy all year round: the maritime museum, the shipwright's, the reception of groups of residents, the open sea music festival are all organised by the team set up by the *département* of the Manche. In summer, when the first fine days arrive, the island opens up to tourists who come for a few hours, to walk and "have a change of air" and see just what this rock looks like, which was completely unknown by many not so long ago.

Close to the little port, on the path leading to the island museum, is the customs officers' house: it is used as a welcome point for walkers. Stop here for a moment, just one, before going further. Stop and look out to sea: in the evening, when the light is softer and Saint-Vaast on the other side of the coast is already fading away in the mist, it is a gift from heaven, a beautiful picture. From the other side of the bay you can see Morsalines, with its old houses on the water's edge, just on the strand, and Saint-Marcouf, the Isle of Birds. Further south: the boats cruise out at sea, between two buoys and three rocks. Little jewel of Tatihou, this small port with its stories of the open sea, we were right not to have abandoned you...

The isle of Tatihou seen from Saint-Vaast-la-Hougue (Manche)

At the foot of the "barracks" and the Vauban tower at Tatihou.

19

Barfleur: a painting

*Barfleur at low tide.
one of the prettiest ports
in France.*

On the east coast, Barfleur is not to be missed: it is one of the prettiest villages in France according to the tourist leaflets. Its reputation is deserved. Some people have no hesitation about calling it the "prettiest Channel port". Even though, as far as we are concerned, we prefer others, Barflour is a hundred times worth the detour.

The port, its fine church with solid architecture, the dwellings all around built of schist and granite, have inspired many artists, not least of whom Boudin or Fouace. The same thing still happens today around the old dock: it is not uncommon to meet a Sunday painter working at his canvas to reproduce the surprising and beautiful landscape. Barfleur is also known for its history: at the time of the conquests, they sailed from here for England. "Guillaume le Batard" was not the last. Alexis de Tocqueville, who owned a property near Barfleur,

wrote "For me, this place is full of memories. Do you know that from the top of the tower I can see the port from where William the Conqueror sailed to conquer England?" Barfleur offers fine walks all around: the Gatteville lighthouse, one of the highest in France with its

2422 - BARFLEUR (Manche)
Le Port et les Quais, le jour de
la Bénédiction de la Mer
(21 Septemre 1924)

365 steps, Tocqueville, the village of Alexis and his elegant château, Cape Levi, a magnificent viewpoint on this tormented coast, the port of Val de Saire.

Barfleur: the port and the
quays, the day when the sea
was blessed,
September 21st 1924.
(Monique Sclaresky collection)

Reminder of Barfleur's "conque-
ring" past in William's time,
the "bastard" and...
King of England.

Above:
Granville: the port gives the town its rhythm.

Below:
Granville: blessing the sea.
(Nelson Cazeils collection)

Granville: the privateer temperament

This is another rock. Another boulder. The Rock is referred to as a landmark loaded with historical memories of privateers of the high seas. The Upper Town, an old town with its narrow streets, overlooks the port which is divided into two. On one side, the yachts, a stronghold for sailors of one day or for ever. On the other side, at the foot of the fish market, boats waiting, the stronghold of hardened seamen, fishermen for clams and whelks.

The Rock re-christened itself, evidence of its re-conversion. It is said that Granville, the Rock, is also the "Monaco of the North". Because there is the rock, because at its feet holiday residents live out peaceful days in their rich villas, with an unobstructed view over the sea. The decor looks just like a soft sepia postcard: the promenade along the sea front, the delightful and slightly retro atmosphere of a sea resort created at the peak of the fashion for sea bathing, the casino and thalassotherapy centre. Those who have not taken the time to potter around the Upper Town and Notre-Dame-du-Cap-Lihou, to peer into the back yards of the fine houses made of Chausey granite, those who have not experienced the ambience of the cafés in the port at dusk, facing the sea, those who have not walked along the Hérel docks or on the Plat Gousset, have never really discovered Granville.

This is not the type of port, not the type of town to give itself to the first comer. The Granvillais are proud of coming from Granville, from their town before coming from Normandy, proud of their roots before being part of the rest of the world. Travellers, fishermen, sailors of all kinds, hardened by the swelling waves, they know what they are talking about when they mention the sea and its storms: the Newfoundland trawlers are never far from their thoughts when they recall memories of another age. The Monaco of the North is anything but a peaceful rock.

"Messieurs les Anglais, fire first" (Battle of Fontenoy, 1745). Granville was born on the rock of a citadel built by the subjects of the "perfidious Albion" to keep a watch on the surroundings, essentially the Mont-Saint-Michel, just opposite across the bay. The Upper Town, favoured by privateers and ship-owners, also remembers the famous battle between the Granvillais and the counter-revolutionaries from Vendée, in the 18th century.

At the "doors" of the portcullis marking the entrance into the old town on the rock, there is a plaque in memory of the "heroic siege" of 1793. It is an understatement to say that the town is built around the sea: captains of the high seas, Newfoundlers, seafarers, merchants... all with the same character hardened by sea water, used to sea spray and ocean adventures. In the old town, spared by the 1944 bombing – apart from an incredible raid by Germans based in Jersey who, well after the Normandy liberation in March 1945, wanted to re-conquer the Rock -, there are old houses which are evidence of earlier times, of riches taken from the sea. These old town houses used to be owned by wealthy ship-builders and one of them is known for being the last refuge of the Chevalier Destouches.

Granville: a Granvillaise.
(Monique Sclaresky collection)

Granville: the small port.
(Nelson Cazeils collection)

174 bis. - GRANVILLE. - Petit Bassin

*Chausey: the archipelago
with 365 boulders.*

*Evening light over Granville
(Manche).*

The Old-Granville museum, located in the "Logis du Roi" (King's Lodging), dating back to the 17th century, recalls the story of these men who left for afar, conquerors of a New World, intrepid fishermen and figures belonging to a land which no longer exists. There are amazing documents here, privateers' warrants, contracts, many models and more than a few pictures.

This is the town, the land of Marin Marie, born in Chausey, naval artist, and of Christian Dior whose house is now a museum, the "Canvas" of the poet Richard Anacréon, a collector

without rival. In the museum named after him, there is the town's "inheritance" of the incredible collection of this art lover, bookseller in Paris and Granvillais by origin. This astonishing collection combines memorabilia of Marie Laurencin, Jean Cocteau, Colette, Dufy, Apollinaire and many others.

In season, the town becomes "touristic", the port is bustling and the sails billow. Here is the "Granvillaise", a fishing smack which is a replica of an old fishing boat from the Mont-Saint-Michel bay, which carries the torch and shows the way. Here, Chausey is never far away; the boulders bordering the big island are the private gardens of yachtsmen and walkers for the pleasure of rediscovering the archipelago of fifty-two rocks when the first fine days arrive. When the tide recedes, they say that Chausey reveals as many boulders as there are days in the year. This must certainly be true, because you can count them until you give up...

At sea, each day brings something new: they sort out the world at the yacht-club bar, and during these evenings it becomes easier to understand Granville and the Granvillais. The privateers have their temperament: they never really left town...

Cherbourg: the mountain is beautiful

The rock gave birth to... a mountain. Here, it is not a matter of a rock, but of a mountain, a really real one, a monument which dominates the roadstead, which looks out over the whole town, nothing but the town.

At about 117 metres above sea level, the view is unbeatable. You must start your pilgrimage and walking from here. The Roule Mount is to Cherbourg what the Rock is to Granville. But without the charm? At least that is what the spiteful say and those who do not understand that a town reveals itself when it is approached and brought out of its shell.

Does this port at land's end have such a bad reputation that everyone prefers other more typical places like Carteret to the west or Barfleur to the east? Beware of appearances. It is well known that they are often deceptive. The military rigidity – here the arsenal is worth a cathedral – the cold appearance of many of the buildings on the edge of town may discourage more than one, certainly. But open the

door, push a bit further, stop for a minute at the top of this strange mountain. The town is at your feet. Its fishing port is further away, and its yacht harbours. Nearby is the former coastguards' building and, on the other side, the locks – the famous turn-bridge – the town is still living on its memories, and the charm remaining.

Is it because of the landscape? Or the history of the town? The Cher-

View over Cherbourg from the Roule Mount.

Cherbourg: the arsenal - the torpedo base.
(Monique Sclaresky collection)

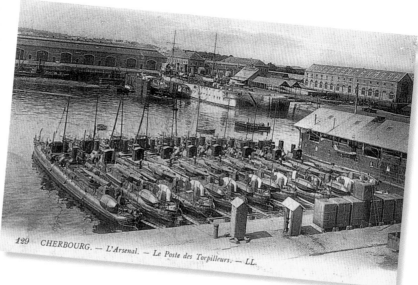

129 CHERBOURG. — L'Arsenal. — Le Poste des Torpilleurs. — LL.

Cherbourg port inside town.

bourgeois are islanders in their soul. The big roadstead must certainly play its part. It was built under Louis XVI who ordered the project from the Civil Engineering expert Louis-Alexandre Cénart. The great sea-wall linked Querqueville Point to Pelée Island. A little later, to defend it, forts had to be built which are still the two landmarks at the entrance to the big roadstead to the east for Pelée island and to the west for Querqueville. The two sea-walls surrounding the whole of the dock were built under the 3rd Republic.

Cherbourg: fishing-boat in dry dock.
(Nelson Cazeils collection)

26

The capital role played by the deep sea port of Cherbourg in the history of the Normandy landings must be remembered. The heaviest material was unloaded here, essential for the Allied forces in their conquest of the territory occupied by the German army. The big roadstead, emblem of the town, is also representative of all its history: the birth of the arsenal, the construction of nuclear submarines here, the arrival of yachting and its expansion, the fabulous era of transatlantic crossings.

Let's stop for a while on this period which left its mark on the Cherbourg townscape. As evidence of these "good" times: the harbour terminal which is going to be turned into a museum, a "sea city". It is a huge building with austere facades, but nonetheless a model of its type: built in the 1930's, it was witness to so many dreams nourished by the idea of a New World, on the other side of the waves. All of Europe's voyagers went through Cherbourg. It is said that, from the end of the 19th century to the first decades of the 20th, more than 70 million passengers passed through the Transatlantic terminal! Just next to the wharf is the former Atlantic Hotel, turned into offices these days, but which was an obligatory stop for emigrants to undergo health checks. The voyage was named after the famous liners: the White Star Line, the

Cunard or the Red Star line carried passengers between the Old Continent and the New World.

The locals admire the "Norway" berthed in Cherbourg.

Sea City

The "Cité de la Mer" *(Sea City)* is a vast touristic, scientific and cultural centre, unique in Europe, and totally devoted to man's underwater adventure. The transatlantic harbour terminal, an exceptional site, will be opened to the public in the year 2001. The partial renovation of a rare monument, and traces of a prestigious past, will be accompanied by building two major centres of interest:

• a dry dock to house the biggest submarine in the world which can be visited: the "Redoutable".

• a permanent Exhibition Hall which, around a new generation cylindrical giant aquarium, will develop scientific and museographic platforms devoted to the understanding of the submarine world after visiting the "Redoutable", and also to the exploitation of underwater biological, industrial and archaeological riches...

525. - Le Paquebot géant " Olympic " de la White Star Line, entrant en Rade de Cherbourg
Transatlantique le plus grand du monde - Longueur 268 mètres, largeur 29 mètres, hauteur du Pont supérieur au dessus de l'eau, 27 mètres
Déplacement 66.000 tonnes - Force 70.000 chevaux

*The giant "Olympic"
liner entering the Cherbourg
roadstead.*
(P. Hennebert collection)

*The jetty marks the entry
to the roadstead.*
(Monique Sclaresky collection)

albums have been printed telling the history of the port facing America. These days, the maritime terminal is for cross-Channel travellers. The ferries going to the south coast of England have replaced the liners with their luxury cabins.

Times change, but memories remain. The statue of Napoleon, at the foot of the Chantereyne docks, shows the Emperor with his arm stretched out towards the open sea. "I decided to renew the marvels of Egypt in Cherbourg". Memory of Saint Helena, the forgotten grandeur of a town which is not without charm for those who are willing to take the time to understand it better.

You can understand it better by remembering the voyages made by a former mayor, Emmanuel Liais: astronomer, botanist, naturalist, he went on a mission to Brazil on behalf of the Paris Observatory, and brought back many tropical plants. His "secret garden", close to the port, has become one of the best known and most appreciated parks in the region. And then there is the Thomas-Henry museum, with its works by Jean-François Millet, the Chantereyne maritime museum, rich in extraordinary bric-a-brac including one of the

In April 1912, Cherbourg was – and for good reason – the first and last stopover of the ill-fated "Titanic". The images of mass departures from here evoke the passage of hundreds of liners, up to more than nine hundred per year which, in the Edwardian era, put in at Cherbourg. The last of them, the "Queen Elisabeth II", which continued to cross the Atlantic long after the others, is also part of these memories today. There remain a few images and numerous souvenirs from previous times. Books and beautiful

lifeboats from the "Nomadic", the ferry which took passengers from the Cherbourg quays to the "Titanic" still in the roadstead, awaiting its fatal voyage, the Charles de Lalande Italian theatre, on Charles-de-Gaulle Square, better known here as "Castle Square", and the Vœu Abbey founded by Mathilde, daughter of Henry I of England. Finally, a short walk away, there is the well-known Ravalet châ- teau, haunted by the memory of Julien and Marguerite, brother and sister accused of incest and beheaded in 1603 on Execution Square.

Is the weather worse here than anywhere else? Everyone talks about Cherbourg's famous umbrellas (the French film *"Les parapluies de Cher- bourg"*). The story was made up by Jacques Demy and filmed with the beautiful Catherine Deneuve. Once again, beware of appearances: Cher- bourg, at the same latitude as the mouth of the Saint Lawrence river in Quebec, benefits from an ocean cli- mate which suits the exotic plants of the Emmanuel Liais garden perfectly.

Certainly, this land's end port is baffling: but after all it is the only one in Normandy built at the foot of... a mountain!

The Ravalet château, Tourlaville.

Vœu Abbey.

races of the cafés, the pubs and rather chic restaurants are crowded. It is fun to eat mussels and chips watching the old riggings dancing in front of half-timbered houses. A postcard picture, a tourist leaflet just for itself, a place loved by walkers, Honfleur is everything at once.

But we cannot forget its splendid history telling of exciting voyages and extraordinary adventurers. Champlain left from Honfleur to found Quebec, on the other side of the high seas. The Sainte-Catherine church, a "cathedral" all on its own, is also evidence of times past. Its outline is worth the visit. Clad in wood, it was

Xavier Leprince.
"Honfleur, loading cattle
on the Passager"
1823. Paris, Louvre Museum.
Photo Giraudon (from "Normandy, the birthplace of Impressionism",
Ouest-France publications, 1999)

Honfleur, the Lieutenancy
and the port.
from "Normandy, the birthplace of
Impressionism",
Ouest-France publications, 1999)

Honfleur, on the jetty.
(Nelson Cazeils collection)

Honfleur:
a pocket-sized port

There is no mountain here, but a steep climb called Mont Joli. There is no big roadstead but a tiny dock looking as though it came out of a miniature world. No submarines, and certainly no liners, but little fishing smacks with memories filled with sea spray.

Honfleur is a world of its own, one of the most popular ports of the coast, one of the most typical, one of the most charming. In season, the promenade along the quays of the old dock has the airs of a high mass. The ter-

built just after the Hundred Years' War. Naval carpenters built the main structure; perhaps this is why, when you cross the threshold, you feel that you are inside a ship. Honfleur life was centred around here beforehand: Sainte-Catherine, with its separate

belfry, the small square and narrow streets, with the dock at the foot.

The walk takes you to the land of Erik Satie and Alphonse Allais in the High Street and of Eugène Boudin, natives of this country. This land was their land, and also belonged to many artists who never tired of the light and the stone: Baudelaire, Flaubert, Monet, Dufy.

Each year, at Whitsun, the Honfleur dock recalls its history: the boats are decorated and covered with flowers and form a procession before being blessed. This is a festive occasion, when the Honfleurais meet each other again, which they appreciate so much. This is the occasion, for those who have left, to revisit the town which has not changed: the wooden houses above the quays, the *Lieutenance*, former dwelling of the King's lieutenant, remains of a building from the 16th century, the salt warehouses, astonishing storehouses from the 17th century with superb timber work.

The pocket-sized port exudes a delicious atmosphere of memories and amusement, perhaps more than any other port in Normandy. Is it because of their presence lurking behind the walls? Alphonse Allais and Erik Satie helped turn these places into a special universe. Alphonse Allais was born on October 20th, 1854 – the same day as Arthur Rimbaud – at 8 Grande-Fontaine square in Honfleur, nowadays called Hamelin square. One of his biographers notes that his first joke on

Honfleur, the old port.

Honfleur; the "native land" of Boudin, Alain and Erik Satie.

Eugène Boudin. "Honfleur Port".
1858-1862.
Paris, Schmit Gallery
(from "Normandy, the birthplace
of Impressionism",
Ouest-France publications, 1999)

arrival in this world was not to talk... for three years. Several years later he could always be found at Mère Toutain's, in the Saint-Siméon farm, rich in memories of an era when Eugène Boudin fixed on canvas "the elegant ladies in crinolines, protecting their delicate complexions with little parasols when they go out on the jetty, a favourite place to walk".

The Satie houses, including the house in the High Street where the composer was born, can be visited these days: they tell of the somewhat bizarre world of the French composer, and his collection of heteroclite objects. You can see the famous monkey automaton, the violin shoe and the harp with barbed wire. Alphonse would have enjoyed this flashback to the past, these abracadabra stories of an unrivalled genius.

The history of the old port and its beautiful houses is all there. And even a little further, as the walk continues. Pause in the Boudin museum, breathe the air of another age and a tremendous passion. Eugène Boudin, native of the place – born on July 12th 1824 in Bourdet street, and long considered, according to his biographers, as a "minor master", was incredibly productive. About four thousand paintings are attributed to him plus seven thousand sketches, among which "only" one hundred and twenty paintings are devoted to his native town and its surroundings. However, it was Honfleur and his meeting with Baudelaire, whose mother lived near the estuary in a "toy house" on the hills above town, which revealed his immense talent in the eyes of his contemporaries including a certain

Courbet who was always filled with amazement. "Few people paint as well as he does", said the artist.

Boudin and the wonderful era of Saint-Siméon must be remembered. At that time, the farm-auberge, which has since become a *"relais-château"*, welcomed many intellectuals and artists who made it their favourite canteen. Mère Toutin took in all this

In the distance, the Seine has grown a bridge between the two banks of Normandy, a strange creature which leaves its imprint on the seaside landscape. The architecture is splendid, incredibly audacious. This little land of Honfleur, its old port, its landscapes from former times, and its antiquated charm, look out over the estuary fashioned by man. A postcard

society around her table. It was here that Boudin found those who were to become his friends: Baudelaire of course but also Corot, Courbet, Sisley, Monet, Millet... and many others. The avant-garde of impressionism was on its way: the lighting and the skies of Honfleur were to become references for ever. One day Claude Monet stated "If I became a painter, I owe it to Boudin". The museum recounts these times. On the second floor, there are several works by the "minor master" who became a great master and two paintings by Monet representing Etretat and Honfleur.

The Grâce coast lives up to its name well. Close by, up in the hills of Honfleur, take your time to appreciate the panorama seen from there. The little chapel built in 1600 is that of the sailors who pray to Our Lady.

which never changes in the slightest, eternal memories of a port from where the adventurers used to sail away. A land with an extraordinary history...

Port-en-Bessin: Sunday market

Another history, another world. This is a small fishing port with a fine promenade above the waves, sheer cliffs dropping into the sea which make you dizzy dominating the world.

In order to discover the surroundings, it is best not to go straight into town. Make the tour of the property, the sea version, lose yourself on the Huppain side where they have created a fashionable golf course in recent years with houses which are

Port-en-Bessin: the fish market.
(Nelson Cazeils collection)

The Sunday promenade: Saint-Bessin quays.

too modern here and there, and carry on to the coast passing the semaphore.

On the other side of the creek, Mont Castel winks an eye, for the pleasure of sailing enthusiasts who, on Sundays in poor weather, have the time of their lives. The town is beneath your feet. A port in the middle of Bessin country, on a coast called the Pearl coast. All around, the beaches tell of the Normandy landings, huge boulders which have witnessed other things, and walks past the coastal resorts which have the antiquated atmosphere of peaceful family holidays. The Bessin is Arromanches, the Pointe du Hoc and the surroundings of Hermanville, Lion-

sur-Mer, Ouistreham, Luc-sur-Mer, Saint-Aubin. Almost all have their own casino, their row of old houses, playgrounds and thalassotherapy centres.

Port-en-Bessin, right in the middle, is the exception, which makes it attractive. No beach, no casino, and what is more no thalasso but a fish auction, the real thing and an armada of boats which set off to fish for shellfish. The early mornings are never sad but on the contrary very animated. Port-en-Bessin is really itself when the sun comes up: the fishermen, tough as nails, carry out their business, the wholesalers test the crates arranged in rows, spread out in the shade of the quays. On the next floor the fishery professionals, where sales are made by computer but in a friendly atmosphere. Watch all this and then go on to the cafe opposite, at the time for coffee and croissants.

Sunday morning is a special day: the market is typical, traditional, and without any doubt one of the most authentic in the region. On Sunday afternoon, take a walk between chocolate buns and water ices. Port-en-Bessin, former oil port during the first days of the liberation of the Normandy beaches, has kept its youthful spirit. A little creek in the sea, a strand at the foot of beautiful cliffs: the departure point for many walks along the coast.

Port-en-Bessin: one of the biggest fishing ports of the Normandy coast.

A Haven of memories

You have to cross over the Seine to go further. The contrast is striking. It can sometimes be upsetting. Drive over the new Normandy bridge, and you reach a quite different landscape, a universe which Marguerite Duras liked to contemplate at nightfall when she stayed on the heights of Trouville. The evening is impressive on the banks of the huge river, at the edge of the estuary: one would think it was another world, another history.

At the mouth, Cape Hève keeps a lookout. Its lighthouse, one of the oldest in France, was the first to be electrified. This was back in 1863, thanks to a steam engine. It could tell many stories. It is the living memory of these places, in past eras: deep sea adventures, the ship building epoch, transatlantic crossings and shipwrecks... It lights up the whole town with its optical memory.

The town was born from... a royal decree. François I was the first to have the idea of building a port to answer the needs of the times. Then, it meant facing England, the hereditary enemy. It was also a matter of preventing the silting up of neighbouring ports, including Harfleur. The choice of "Le Havre de Grâce" (Haven of Grace) was important. Here the high tide lasts for two hours, a "natural" element which later counted a great deal for the future of the port.

Its heart dithered between defence and business. Richelieu and then Colbert fortified it while trade developed with territories from the other end of

Le Havre: fishermen.
(Nelson Cazeils collection)

Le Havre: The Pilots' cove.
(Nelson Cazeils collection)

280. LE HAVRE — Effets de Vagues à la nouvelle Jetée
Waves appearance on the New Pier

Le Havre: waves against the jetty.
(Monique Sclaresky collection)

Le Havre: crab collectors after a high tide.
(Nelson Cazeils collection)

the world, India and China in particular. Time went by and shaped the landscape around. Life in Le Havre turned around deep-sea fishing, whale hunting, ship building, transatlantic liners, coffee, cotton and the slave trade! In 1518 the first warship entered the port: the "Hermine" was the first of a long, a very long, series of ships, cargo boats, cruise boats which, little by little and more and more, adopted it as their home port.

Le Havre is not quiet: it stretches over more than 2,500 acres of docks and can count some 18 miles of quays. The traffic is colossal: over fifty million tons of goods are loaded or unloaded every year. Do not be put off by its architecture nor the austere landscapes and refineries all around. Don't just think that it is a place to be avoided. The town was destroyed on the threshold of re-conquered freedom – it was one of the most damaged of all of Normandy during the 1944 bombing. Behind the walls redesigned by Auguste Perret, chief architect in charge of rebuilding, a character was forged soaked in seawater; peaceful resorts, and memories drenched by sea spray.

When the "Norway", formerly the "France" docked alongside the quays not so long ago, there was a huge celebration shared by thousands of Havrais, big and little. It was as if the blessed era of ocean liners counted more here than elsewhere. Le Havre was the port for the giants, departure point for dream cruises, ideas of grandeur, luxury, gangways. The place was nicknamed the "Ocean Port". This says everything, tells everything about what the coming and going of the great liners meant for the locals.

The Maritime and Port museum, in the former Vauban docks, recounts

York and at its zenith, before the last War, was the biggest and finest of ships.

The sea front, a delightful wind-swept promenade, was witness to this wonderful history. It also tells of all the charm of a town which one learns to know, little by little. In order to discover it better, a good address: Sainte-Adresse. Above the port, in the direction of the Hève Cape, this chic promontory was the summer resort for a good number of artists, painter and writers, who dreamed of travels and departures.

This is the throne of the "sugar-loaf" cenotaph, a form of homage erected by the widow of General

Left:
**The "Norway" arrives
in the port of Le Havre.**

**Le Havre now has
2,500 acres of docks.**

the history of ocean liners and doc-kers. Souvenirs, sad souvenirs some-times: the Le Havre naval shipyards, - called the ACH – built some of the most beautiful and biggest liners here including the well known "Club Med" series. Many years after the great crossings, the memories are preser-ved here jealously, by creating collec-tions. Some are specialised in objects linked with famous crossings: the crockery of the "France", models of the "Normandy", ashtrays from the "Liberty", the presents which the General Transatlantic Company of-fered its passengers. From time to time, these cult objects are put on auction: buyers sometimes come from very far away, essentially from the United States, to recuperate pieces of a puzzle which is above all sentimental. Apart from the "France", it is the "Normandy" which catches the imagination here: it plied the route Le Havre-Southampton-New

Le Havre: the transatlantic "Léopoldina".
(Monique Sclaresky collection)

Etretat and its famous "needle".

Hève lighthouse or the semaphore it is easy to imagine how the beautiful skies, the gentle landscapes, and the play of light influenced the painters. Eugène Boudin, a neighbour from Honfleur, found the major reason to hope for better days in this town. Le Havre provided him with the financial support needed for his early work as an artist. Raoul Dufy, native of this land, discovered here such a "lesson of light" that he founded the group of the Fauve movement, along with Georges Braque and others. "I was carried away by the light over the estuaries." It is essential to go and see the works of the masters on display here at the Beaux-Arts museum.

Lefebvre-Desnouettes who disappeared at sea off Iceland in 1822. It is a landmark dedicated to passing sailors just like the little chapel to the east nearby, Notre-Dame-des-Flots, rich in ex-votos and its fine prayer-book. For Le Havre, Sainte-Adresse is the memory of sea bathing and rich villas lived in by celebrities in earlier times. The "rock" is also part of the history of the town: during the First World War it sheltered the Belgian Government in exile!

Walking up and down the roads, following the beach, climbing up to the

Le Havre is not far from the banks of Lower-Normandy. The Normandy bridge astride the estuary brought neighbours closer together who, previously, had watched each other from a distance. They say that it is the occasion to rediscover a whole and indivisible Normandy. Between the Upper and the Lower, there is an anchor point, a haven making the junction. This port also represents the history of these "two worlds"...

Etretat:
the gentleman burglar

This again is a picture postcard, scenery out of a novel. Not a port but "doors" as Maupassant wrote. "The beach, with its famous beauty so often depicted by painters, seems like a fairyland decor with its two marvellous fissures in the cliff which are called doors." Everything has been said already, but no one ever tires of saying it again.

You have to climb the Amont cliff to discover the amazing panorama. The shingle beach is just below with the Aval cliff with its famous "needle" behind. The first attempt to cross the Atlantic on wings took off from this rocky point plunging into the water. The monument erected in memory of Nungesser and Coli is a reminder of the saga of the beautiful "White Bird" which was never found again.

The novelist Alphonse Karr, who frequented Sainte-Adresse, made the place known. Etretat inspired many writers, beginning with Maupassant who spent part of his childhood here. Arsène Lupin also found "refuge" here! His creator, Maurice Leblanc, made the hollow Needle the hideout of his fetish character. The Clos Lupin, the house which was formerly the property of the author, reminds passing tourists of the strange story of the "gentleman burglar".

Just next to Etretat, ten miles to the north, you must see Yport, a pretty seaside resort, nestled in a little valley in the Alabaster Coast, between two cliffs of the Caux country. This minuscule port is built on memories of the time when they sailed off to fish for whiting, turbot and herring.

Yport, back from fishing (Seine-Maritime).

Yport fisherman.

Le Littoral
26. - FÉCAMP.- Départ pour Terre-Neuve.

*Fécamp: departure for
Newfoundland.*
(Nelson Cazeils collection)

*Fécamp: everything recalls
the sea and fabulous
ocean adventures.*

Fécamp: herring
and a drop of milk

The Virgin keeps watch, like at Le Havre and Honfleur, like at most other places along the coast. Here the hill is named after her and you have to climb up the sailors' path to discover the beauty of the scenery and absorb the atmosphere it exudes. Welcome to Fécamp, an obligatory

stopping place for those wishing to walk along the Alabaster Coast.

There is the little chapel of Notre-Dame-de-Salut at the top of the "Virgin's hill". It overlooks the port, far down, perched on one of the highest cliffs of the coast. At 110 metres above sea-level, the panorama is impressive. The chapel tells the story of this bit of the coast: it is said that it was the scene of violent battles during the Wars of Religion and, to save the ruin, they had to support its vaulting with ships' masts. These days it acts as a landmark for sailors and fishermen, which is only justice.

Here, the sea means everything. In the smallest lanes, the little paths, up to the chimneys of the old *"boucanes"* where they smoked the fish. In French, Fécamp rhymes with herring (hareng). The Newfoundlanders have their museum here and some visitors come from far away to discover the history of their ancestors, fishermen who ventured as far as the icy waters of Newfoundland to seek their fortune.

North of the Saint-Lawrence river, five hours by plane from Montreal, there is a maritime museum on a rock imprisoned in the ice each winter, which recounts this same story. In the Madeleine islands, a bit of Quebec, they have a special tenderness for Fécamp and its fishermen. "Cousin" relations have been woven on each side of the Atlantic and the Quebec museum devotes several showcases to souvenirs of its ancestors from Normandy.

The name of Fécamp takes its origin from the term "pisk" which turns into "fish" in English. The Newfoundlanders and Fishing museum on the quays is an institution here. Right from the Middle Ages, the "hareng de Fescan" had a good reputation throughout the kingdom of France. The town and its port developed around fishing: at the beginning of the 20th century, there were no fewer than two thousand five hundred Fécampois fishermen who sailed away for

The native land of the old Newfoundlanders.

The herring season at Fécamp (December): bringing in the catch.
(Nelson Cazeils collection)

Fécamp: view of the worksite.
(Nelson Cazeils collection)

Wooden jetties were built and, much later, works were started including wet docks.

Since then nothing, or almost nothing, has changed. You can find the astonishing souvenirs of a doctor ahead of his time: it is here that Léon Dufour, who came from Saint-Lô, "invented" the famous "drop of milk", an organisation intended to fight against infant mortality. His work, to be seen in Precious-Blood Street (a whole programme!) made the tour of the world, helping young mothers often coming from poor families to receive sterilised milk for their babies. The "child pavilion" retraces the fabulous story of the doctor for the poor who made Fécamp a model of its type.

Behind the port, you can discover the great adventure of Benedictine and its creator, Alexandre Le Grand, a wine merchant from Fécamp who

long seasons, from the last days of winter to the middle of the summer months. Later, the big trawlers went back and forth between the Great North and the port in Normandy: the cod was salted and frozen on board ship before being brought back to port. These days, cod fishing has

The port has undergone many transformations.

disappeared but the smokehouses remain. Here they are called *"sauris-series"* where they still cure herrings over beech shavings.

Work was carried out on the port until the end of the 19th century. Henry II Plantagenet, Duke of Normandy and King of England, donated it to the Benedictine monks who were the first to begin organising the site, making a barrier between the port and the marshy area, in the estuary.

was at the origin of the famous liqueur which a Venetian monk, dom Bernardo Vincelli, invented. The monk's elixir carries a special note which is always to be found on the bottles of the precious alcohol: DOM, that is Deo Optimo Maximo (To God, the very great, the very good). The Benedictine museum here is a "palace": to such an extent that the liqueur left its mark on the spirit and scene of the town.

Earlier, and not so long ago, the "sailors' path" was taken by sailors climbing up the cliff on their knees or with bare feet. They came from the wet docks to ask protection from Our Lady. The "path" is still there. It is the memory of this land which forgets nothing of its past and, even better, cares for it, around its docks, the Dukes' Palace, the Abbey and the little chapel of Notre-Dame. High up there, on the top of the cliff.

Dieppe: ivory and sea bathing

This is another story. Another type of fishing, another port. The sea is there, right in the centre of town, and all around there are memories of fishing for shellfish. The castle dominates everything, from above the port, and you must go up there to discover the town. Here, the ivory route takes on all its meaning. In the middle of the 16th century, seafarers from here brought back such a quantity of ivory that they created a commerce employing craftsmen, and traces can still be found today.

Dieppe: the ivory trail has its roots here.

Dieppe: the harbour terminal: a liner arriving.
(Monique Sclaresky collection)

*Dieppe: fishermen
at Le Pollet.*
(Nelson Cazeils collection)

Normandy fisherwoman.
(Nelson Cazeils collection)

In Dieppe they continue to work ivory and the Dieppe museum devotes a very large section to it. Fishing, travel, craftsmen, adventure... and sea-bathing. The town never forgets that it is the oldest sea resort along the coast. And it has proof: in 1578, King Henri III came here to bathe "to cure certain itches" and later Madame de Sévigny reported that ladies of the Court went there to have a quick dip. Queen Hortense of Holland, related to Napoleon I, followed the example and it was the Duchesse de Berry who really started the big fashion for sea-bathing: between 1824 and 1830, she spent a large part of her holidays here, bringing a good number of her aristocrat friends with her.

The sea is everything here. The town is huddled around the estuary. The Arques, the river from the Caux country, already served as refuge for fishermen looking for a peaceful mooring place, right back in ancient times. Everyone followed their example. Dieppe has a privileged situation: William the Conqueror, when he became King of England, helped its development. Later the followers of François I trimmed their sails and left from Dieppe in search of new countries and new treasures.

Ango, the ship-owner, remains famous round here because of his arsenal "which made kings tremble". He set off to fight the Portuguese sailors, and polished them off in no time. It was one his ships, under the command of the Parmentier brothers, which was the first to cross the mythical line of the equator. It was another of his ships which, in 1524, first discovered the site in America now called New York. Not far from here, at Varengeville, the house where Ango lived still stands, a magnificent wooden palace with Italian-style decoration.

*Dieppe: **loading the nets*** (Nelson Cazeils collection).

The port for all the voyagers was also that of artists, writers, painters, musicians. From among those who passed through Dieppe or stayed there, we can pick out Jacques-Emile Blanche who was born there and whose work is a landmark. We can also mention the presence of Degas, Renoir, Monet or Gauguin, rediscover the texts of Alain the philosopher, and the music of Saint-Saëns whose last concert took place in Dieppe.

Caux country,
the source of inspiration
for very many painters.

More recently, the town was the scene of a real massacre, a prelude to the Allied landings in 1944. Two years before, English and Canadian forces

The castle, "central square" of the Pollet district.

had attempted a landing with terrible memories: 7,000 men took part in the Dieppe raid during the night of August 19th 1942. But the continuous heavy fire of the German batteries forced them to withdraw, not without difficulty; a resounding defeat.

These days, the peaceful town recalls its history quietly: at the foot of the castle, around the Pollet district and in the shadow of Saint-Rémy, a compromise between Gothic and Renaissance architecture, and of Saint-Jacques the main parish, the memory of ivory and ocean-going

voyages predominates. Dieppe, close to England, is now the departure point for new, swift, Channel crossings. Inside the museum, the carved ivory, the paintings by Jacques-Emile Blanche and the memories of Camille Saint-Saëns are a good way of understanding quickly this northern town and its surroundings "one of the most beautiful spectacles offered by Nature".

Le Tréport: Victor's wings

"There, you can feel the fluttering of wings", wrote Victor Hugo. "If I did not have my nest in Paris, I would take off." He was talking about his stay in Le Tréport, about the cliff dominating the town and which makes it even smaller than it is and perhaps prettier. The "Terrasses" are a unique viewpoint. A long staircase – over 370 steps – leads from Town Hall square up to the summit, there where Victor Hugo felt wings sprouting behind him.

In Le Tréport, the quays are the history of the town. They stretch along narrow roads, bordered by café and restaurant terraces. The town was founded in the 9th century and Robert I founded the Benedictine Abbey of Saint-Michel here, which no longer exists. A glance at the Normandy landscape: they

Le Tréport: entering the jetties.
(Nelson Cazeils collection)

wanted to close the loop between the Mont Saint-Michel in the bay to the south and this abbey in the north which marks the border and extremity of the whole of Normandy.

The port has been transformed several times: Vauban modified it, and the jetty was extended in the 19th century. Le Tréport is known for its fishing, its former merchant activities and its...shingles. Did you know that the rocket launch pad of Cape Canaveral in the United States is made of shingles from round here? Searching for shingles used to be an institution: many families lived off it, going out on the beaches or at the foot of the cliffs, to hunt for these stones polished by the sea. They made crockery or ornaments out of them. Le Tréport is a little nest, a darling of a port, a pretty creek in the sea. Here the landscape is made up of cliffs with impressive outlines which Sunday walkers love to gaze at. No one ever tires of the astonishing spectacle of the sea beating

against the sides of these "mountains" which are amongst the highest along the coast. High up, the wayside cross of the Terrasses makes you want to set off for walks. Victor Hugo was not wrong: we are only missing the wings...

Le Tréport: the town must be looked at from the top of the "dead cliff".
(Photo Richard Nourry, from "The Customs Officers' Paths in Normandy", Editions Ouest-France, 1997).

Le Tréport: hunting for crabs.
(Nelson Cazeils collection)

L'Hirondelle

The garden route

Enclosed gardens or sumptuous parks, flowerbeds or exotic greenhouses: the gardens of Normandy are a pure delight. There are amazing stories hiding behind each corner of greenery...

NAQUEVILLE (Manche): a sea view

This is a picture recognised by every enthusiast of verdure and fine buildings. A 16th century château surrounded by a romantic park, with a river running through, with waterfalls and flowery fountains. The perfect decor for those entering the kingdom of the parks and gardens of the Cotentin. The park of the Nacqueville château directly overlooks... the sea.

The landscape is astonishing when you enter, facing the ocean, full of rhododendrons, azaleas, hydrangeas and giant gunnera.

Left:
Giverny, Trimming the water lilies in the water garden.

Park of the château of Nacqueville.

Special garden
Religious building
Château

0　　　　30 km

Le Tréport

Eu

SOMME
80

L A   M A N C H E

Varengeville

Dieppe

St-Valery-en-Caux

Offranville

Château
de Miromesnil

Neufchâtel-
en-Bray

Parc
Emmanuel Liais

Château de
Nacqueville

St-Germain-
des-Vaux

La Roche
Fauconnière

Cap de la Hague

Nez de Jobourg

Cap
Lévy

Pointe de
Barfleur

Cap d'Antifer

Yport

Fécamp

Étretat

CÔTE D'ALBÂTRE

P A Y S   D E   C A U X

76

Bosmelet

Jardins de
Bellevue

St-Saëns

Jardin
de Vauville

Vauville

Cherbourg

Barfleur

Tôtes

Clères

Agapanthe
Clos du Coudray

Cap de
Flamanville

Martinvast

Château de
Martinvast

St-Vaast-la-Hougue

Yvetot

Bolbec

Les Forrières
du Bosc

Gournay-
en-Bray

Valognes

St-Marcouf

Le Havre

SEINE-
MARITIME

Jardin
des Plantes

Montmain

OISE
60

C O T E N T I N

Barneville-
Carteret

Cap de Carteret

Ste-Mère-Église

Pointe
du Hoc

Cap de la Hève

CÔTE DE NACRE

Honfleur

Seine

ROUEN

Vandrimare

Gisors

Les Andelys

Isigny-
sur-Mer

Arromanches-
les-Bains

St-Aubin-sur-Mer

Deauville

CÔTE
FLEURIE

Pont-Audemer

Elbeuf

Louviers

Carentan

Bayeux

Luc-sur-Mer

Ouistreham

Pont-l'Évêque

Arboretum
d'Harcourt

Vernon

VAL-
D'OISE
95

Périers

Plantbessin

Creully

Château
de Brécy

Jardin des
Plantes

Cambremer

Lisieux

Le Neubourg

Évreux

Villers-
Fossard

Castillon

Colline aux
Oiseaux

CAEN

N 13

Bernay

Giverny

YVELINES
78

Agon-Coutainville

Pointe d'Agon

Coutances

Saint-Lô

Villers-Bocage

Mézidon-Canon

Château de Canon

Orbec

EURE

27

MANCHE

14

St-Pierre-sur-Dives

Beaumesnil

Conches-sur-
Ouche

Îles
Chausey

CALVADOS

Château de
Vendeuvre

Crouttes

Vimoutiers

Pointe du Roc

Granville

la Haye-
Pesnel

Vire

Cerisy-
Belle-Étoile

Falaise

Prieuré
Saint-Michel

Villers-
en-Ouche

L'Aigle

Nonancourt

Pointe de Champeaux

Villedieu-
les-Poêles

Flers

61

Argentan

Gacé

Verneuil-
sur-Avre

26
EURE-
ET-LOIR

Baie du Mont-
Saint-Michel

Avranches

Mortain

ORNE

Château de
Sassy

St-Christophe-
de-Jajolet

Sées

Manoir de
Pontgirard

le Mont-St-Michel

Pontorson

St-Hilaire-
du-Harcouët

Domfront

La Ferté-Macé

Mortagne-
au-Perche

35
ILLE-ET-
VILAINE

53
MAYENNE

Alençon

72
SARTHE

Bellême

28
EURE-
ET-LOIR

It was an English landscape gardener who gave it its letters patent of nobility: in 1830 he designed the park of the château where Hippolyte de Tocqueville lived, the brother of Alexis, to create an expanse entirely devoted to the beauty of plants and flowers. This very romantic park extends over about 90 acres and the species found here exude a delicious exotic atmosphere.

The park is open from Easter to September.

CHERBOURG (Manche): the Cotentin palm trees

A little bit of greenery representing a long voyage. It is named after its creator; botanist and adventurer. Emmanuel Liais was an astronomer and

naturalist, and fascinated by plants from the other end of the world: in 1852, he took part in the creation of the Cherbourg Scientific Society and, two years later, was delegated to the Paris Observatory which sent him to Brazil to found the Rio Astronomy Observatory, which he directed from 1870 to 1881.

This man, who had also been mayor of Cherbourg, brought back many rare and obviously exotic plants from his stay in Brazil. His garden, in the Bucaille district, is an initiation which makes observers say that in Cherbourg the palm trees are ready to replace... the umbrellas. A specialised magazine "Pays de Normandie" described Emmanuel Liais' park very well as the "Tropics of Cotentin", calling it "certainly the most successful of Cherbourg gardens".

However, it is not the only one: another garden is worth the detour, even though it is rarely open to visitors (only six times a year), and this is the "Roche Fauconnière" garden which contains one of the biggest specialised vegetal collections. This "extraordinary" garden holds about 4,000 different species coming from the four corners of the earth.

Above:
La Roche-Fauconnière.

Opposite:
The Emmanuel-Liais park in Cherbourg.

Inland from the dunes of the Hague, the Vauville "paradise".

of the Maritime Hospital here have very many palm trees, pines and gunnera of extraordinary dimensions. The town can count more than 500 palm trees in its various gardens, the Emmanuel-Liais park, the public garden on the Avenue de Paris and the Maritime Hospital garden. Spoilt for choice... to dream of other countries.

VAUVILLE (Manche): garden tools

It is worth the detour just for itself. Because Vauville is the Hague, because the Hague is the wind and this little bit of land resembles Ireland like two drops of water and three stones. Vauville is nestled behind the dunes and the rocks, close to the Joburg "nose" on the west coast of the Cotentin. The garden of the château was created in 1947 by the parents of the present owner. Today, Guillaume Pellerin is carrying on the tradition with great pleasure and keeps it up through his enthusiasm and his collections: he owns an astonishing variety of gardening bric-a-brac, one of the finest and biggest collections of garden tools. The Vauville garden is a "must": more than 700 species from the southern hemisphere are labelled here, and they are recognised as a unique and amazing collection.

The park can be visited from May 1st to October 1st on Sundays and Tuesdays. In June, July and August it is open on Saturdays, Sundays and Tuesdays, and accepts groups upon request.

It is the work of the Favier family, and after the Second World War especially the outlines were laid down which remain today. The work of Charles Favier, country doctor, traveller and in love with plants, has born its fruits: he made endless journeys to the other ends of the world, from Chile to Tasmania, via South Africa and New Zealand, to look for the rarest plants which would adapt to the climate of North Contentin. From "Cornus controversa variegata", originally from China, to trees from Chile, the garden is full of astonishing finds.

The garden side of Cherbourg will never cease to amaze us: the borders

MARTINVAST (Manche): Beaurepaire...

The château is well named: Beaurepaire (Beautiful retreat). The original building dates back to the 14th century but it was altered and then rebuilt in the 19th century. The keep still remains from early times and bears the marks of an ancient epoch. The château is known for its 250-acre park. Water is an important element and the presence of many exotic

*Park of the château of
Beaurepaire at Martinvast.*

varieties of trees is due to Baron de
Schicler who planted the species you
can see here today: sequoias, tulip
trees, cypress, palms, plane trees,
American oaks, rhododendrons. At
the beginning of the 19th century, the
marshes surrounding the château
were transformed into a park inspired
by English landscapes and comprising meadows, pools, forests and
waterfalls. The park is known for its
exemplary collection of exotic
conifers.

*The park is open from April to
November (except Saturdays in April
and October).*

VILLIERS-FOSSARD – SAINT-LÔ
(Manche):
follow the trail

This is an initiation trail teaching
about flowers, plants and trees. However, here there is plenty to occupy
you for a certain time in discovering
several rare trees. At Villiers-Fossard,

at the gates of Saint-Lô, the master of
the house is a nursery gardener who
will give you valuable advice. At the
end of the visit, do not hesitate to ask
him for a few ideas; he will be only
too pleased to help. The park, water
gardens and plantations, offer over
2,500 varieties of plants, trees and
bushes situated according to selected
themes. All along the discovery path,
a sort of floral trail becomes a delightful labyrinth. A real garden on a
human scale, which will make you
dream about what you yourself could
do with a little inspiration from here,
on your own plot of land.

*Open from February to the end of
November.*

SAINT-GERMAIN-DES-VAUX
(Manche):
the soul of the poet

This is not the garden of the little
house at Omonville-la-Petite where
Janine and Jacques Prévert lived.

The childhood home of Christian Dior at Granville.

However, it resembles the poet, who fell in love with the Cotentin and the landscapes of the Hague. This little corner of verdure, at Saint-Germain-des-Vaux, next door to Port-Racine, is entirely devoted to him. It is a sign of friendship and homage to the artist who now rests in the Omonville cemetery, overlooking the sea. One of Prévert's friends, an antique dealer in the Hague, decided to design it and keep it in order. As Prévert said "the countryside is not ugly, perhaps it is your eye which is poor". Prévert's friends planted several pretty bushes in remembrance: a weeping pear, a blue thuya... and other plants as witness of eternal love.

Open every day.

GRANVILLE (Manche): the fashionable garden

This is like a suspended garden. Above the Plat Gousset, the promenade for the inhabitants of Granville, fashion has its flower beds. The Rhums villa is known because it was the childhood home of Christian Dior. The house was acquired by his family, originally from Saint-Sauveur-le-Vicomte, in 1905 and then resold to the town of Granville in 1935. It was Christian Dior's mother who designed the terrace, the winter garden and the pergola. These days you can walk round and at the same time enjoy a unique panorama over the open sea. The Dior family hewed a path into the cliff itself leading down to the strand. The whole house has become a museum devoted to fashion and the garden is being renovated: it is to be returned to its original appearance which was apparently a real English-type garden.

PLANTBESSIN-CASTILLON (Calvados): budding gardeners

You are halfway between Bayeux and Saint-Lô, somewhere in the shade of the fine Balleroy forest which is also called "Cerisy" forest. The spot is

The Christian Dior park.

charming. And the mistress of the house is just as charming. Colette Sainte-Beuve will certainly welcome you between two trips to her flower borders. You cannot find anyone more enthusiastic. Colette Sainte-Beuve calls herself a "collector" rather than a nursery gardener and admits that she has limitless admiration for perennials. Budding gardeners and those in search of advice rush here when the good weather comes. The garden, right next to the "nursery", is a model of its type. It is like a plant version of Ali Baba's cave. However, the "clutter" hides seven borders each based on a theme including a very pretty water garden, a fine alley bordered by wisteria and a landscaped garden.

The speciality of the house is the geranium, Colette Sainte-Beuve's great passion. Plantbessin sells about 2,500 varieties, some of which are very rare. Here usefulness and pleasure go together in perfect harmony accompanied by the delicate perfume of freshly cut flowers.

Open every day except Sunday (the garden in season).

CHÂTEAU DE BRÉCY
(Calvados):
a view over the terraces

Right in the middle of Bessin, close to the landing beaches, this garden is a marvel. It is said to be the creation of François Mansart at the beginning of the 17th century, although no one is really certain. It is a little jewel of greenery and spreads over five independent terraces. The whole is conjugated with talent and elegance: the box trees, the flowers, the lawns which marry Renaissance, medieval and French styles and lead to the foot of the beautiful house which is surrounded by the park behind closed walls. A fine discovery and fine work. And what does it matter whether Mansart was the creator or not...

Open from April to October.

Five independent terraces compose the splendid Brécy garden.

CAEN (Calvados)
BOTANICAL GARDEN:
green spaces

Do the youngsters playing in the sand pit, next to the greenhouses where the tropical plants grow, imagine that they have a rendezvous with history here? There is nothing to prove it. And yet.

In the very centre of the town, close to the "Fossés Saint-Julien", this is a little bit of history as well as a haven of verdure. The *"jardin des plantes"* the botanical garden of the town of Caen, was created in 1736 by... the university! Jean-Baptiste Caillard, originally a professor from the Faculty of Medicine, began to take interest in the plants he was growing in his garden, to aid his teaching.

His successor, François Marescot, followed in his footsteps and became fascinated by flowers, to such an extent that he collected about 600 different species. The university acquired a garden and allowed him to look after his collection and to extend it. After the Revolution, the garden became a park of 10 acres with about 3,500 species and later was enriched by two greenhouses and an orangery.

Above and opposite:
Six thousand plant species in the fine "botanical garden" in the centre of Caen.

These days, it is a pure marvel with more than 6,000 species of plants carefully tended by the Municipal gardeners. The garden also houses the Conservatory of Normandy plants, a medicinal border and many collections of perennials and bi-annuals. A walk here is such a pleasure, and children enjoy it.

Open all year round.

CAEN (Calvados)
LA COLLINE AUX OISEAUX:
refuse with the scent of roses

A daring challenge: make a garden on a pile of refuse and...succeed. This is really a special place, a former waste tip, on the edge of town just next to the Peace Memorial, converted into a garden which is still young but already extraordinary. It was inaugurated on the fiftieth anniversary of the Normandy landings, and the hill owes its name (Bird Hill) to the fact that previously this tip was the refuge of ... seagulls!

There are no more seagulls or hardly any, no more refuse but a wonderful rose garden which, in season, no one can tire of admiring. The alley leading to it is bordered with wisteria and pretty rose bushes. Just next door, there is a box-tree maze which children enjoy and, further on and behind, a lake reached through a series of theme and exotic gardens devoted to the different towns twinned with the capital of Lower Normandy. The park extends over fifty acres and is a delightful place for a walk, for a breath of fresh air. The circular rose garden can count 15,000 bushes, both old and modern varieties. It is worth climbing the hill, just for them.

Open all year round.

"Bird Hill":
a successful reconversion
and a lovely rose garden.

Patchwork of dahlias.

CHÂTEAU DE CANON
(Calvados):
at the foot of the wall

The Caen plain is close, gloomy and somewhat sad. But, nonetheless, this nest is a thousand times worth the detour, even though it was severely damaged by the storm in December 1999. The park of the Canon château is a marvel of its type, a model garden in the pure tradition of the 18th century.

It is an Anglo-French park, the achievement of Elie de Beaumont, who had no hesitations about disturbing the order established around the fine property designed by Le Nôtre. There are Italian statues, a Chinese kiosk, isolated plots which are really vegetable gardens enclosed by walls, inspired by the King's vegetable garden in Versailles. The height of the walls protecting the borders was calculated in function of each location, so as to guarantee the best period of sunlight for the plants. This is a work of art and evidence of real refinement.

Open from Easter to the end of June at weekends and every day from July 1st to September 30th, except Tuesdays.

CHÂTEAU DE VENDEUVRE
(Calvados):
a garden... in miniature

The property has never left the family. Alexandre de Vendeuvre, King's engineer, was the first to live in these premises, which were built for him in 1750. Today, his descendants look after the site and have redesigned the garden, taking their inspiration from the original plans but reserving a few surprises for visitors. Thus the water garden is cunning and when the passer-by admires it, sprays several water jets! There is also a grotto with thousands of sea shells, a Chinese pavilion and behind this a

Top:
Canon: the garden and art...

Bottom:
Shade from the huge trees of Canon.

maze of yews and roses. The Van-deuvre château, specialised in minia-ture objects - there is a very fine col-lection of tiny furniture here - luckily had bigger ideas for its garden.

SASSY (Orne): Saint Christophe, pray for us

This is one of our favourites among all the others around: for the beauty of the location, for the château, for the park, for the terraces and for the walks it inspires. The Sassy château at Saint-Christophe-de-Jajolet, at the border between the Orne and the Cal-vados, is a beautiful spot. It has belon-ged to the Audifret-Pasquier family for five generations. Inside the 18th century property, you discover the history of this big family which has given Lower Normandy one of its most beautiful parks.

The paradise of miniatures, the "speciality" of Vendeuvre.

The Sassy terrace. In the background, the orangery.

Achille Duchêne, taking his inspiration from Le Nôtre, designed the garden where the former vegetable garden used to be. The charm can be appreciated from the Italian-style terraces overlooking it. It is one of the finest examples of a "jardin à la

Above left:
Borders with box-trees in the park of Sassy château.

Above right:
One of the best examples of a "jardin à la française".

française": it consists of several borders, decorated with box-tree whose outlines can be seen against a base of crushed brick and rose-coloured sand, a discerning reminder of the tones of the château's facade. At the end of the garden is the orangery, a little marvel.

But the garden is not the only thing here. The domain extends over 2,500 acres of meadows, woods and a park rich in superb blue cedars, arranged around the château, a stud and a farm. The guided visit is worth it: you will learn that the beautiful building has at least twenty-six bedrooms and fifteen bathrooms, and that the private library collected by Grand Chancellor Pasquier, minister under the Empire, Louis XVIII and Louis-Philippe is the biggest private library in France! Here, within these old walls, the Duke of Edin-

burgh was on a private visit when he learned about the death of Lord Mountbatten.

Saint-Christophe-de-Jajolet is a walk back in time and surprisingly relaxing. The little commune in the Orne is also known for another story: in July each year, drivers come here on a pilgrimage to pray to their patron saint and protector! The beautiful gardens of Sassy really lead to everything...

Open every day, from Easter to All Saints.

PONTGIRARD (ORNE): a garden reborn

Pleasures can be combined. Rediscover the history of a manor several centuries old and clear everything around it, left to abandon. This is the interesting story of Pontgirard, just outside Mortagne-au-Perche: a manor from the 16th century and its reborn garden.

After renovating the buildings, work on the borders began only a few years ago. This rehabilitation is due to the owner, Philippe Siguret, born in the Perche, former inspector general of sites for the Historical Monuments administration and former regional director for cultural affairs. "The Perche is a rural region but the taste for ornamental gardens is deeply rooted", he says. This is why the Pontgirard garden is in the image of an initiation circuit which leaves you to discover, just for the pleasure, the most varied of species. You pass from an alley of euphorbia to an aromatic garden with, further on, a pergola of honeysuckle and clematis.

These expanses are joined by another: a line of little waterfalls which is planned to become the garden of the "five senses". The alley of ash trees, the herb garden, the collection of euphorbia... all planned with care and well looked after, make the visit particularly attractive. The garden is only just at its beginnings, but all of them are promising.

Open on Saturdays, Sundays and bank holidays from May 1st to November 1st.

THE SAINT-MICHEL PRIORY (Orne): salons and roses

We are right in the middle of the Auge country. The priory dates back to the 13th century while the gardens are from the... 20th. They are arranged within a bower of hornbeams and hold a collection of roses, iris, vegetables and perennials, without forgetting the orchard. There is an alley of lime trees all around. The rose garden designed by Louis Benech comprises four "salons", each with one colour predominating; white, pink, yellow

Saint-Michel Priory.

The gardener's companions.

and red. Saint-Michel-des-Crouttes, between Vimoutiers and Argentan, is as well known for its gardens and priory as for the conferences organised here. Enthusiasts of fine gardens, those in love with pretty bouquets and rare plants gather here for talks about gardens. There are also many exhibitions of sculptures, engravings and photographs.

Open Saturdays, Sundays and bank holidays in May, June, and from September 1st to 20th. Open every day except Tuesdays in July and August.

CERISY-BELLE-ETOILE (Orne): king rhodo

This is the homeland of rhododendrons. There are thousands of them – between 4,000 and 5,000 – and people come from far away to see them, close to Flers. Cerisy was born under a lucky star. A former officer in the Indian army, lawyer in London, fell in love with the site and, in 1870, built a château on the hill, of neo-gothic inspiration. In 1955 the local town hall inherited the domain which extends over 250 acres and is said to receive more than 100,000 visitors every year. In May, when the rhododendrons are in flower, it is a real paradise, a wonder for the eyes. On the last weekend of the month, they celebrate the prince of gardens and this is a fête which flower-lovers would not miss for anything.

VILLERS-EN-OUCHE (Orne): grilles of fate

Once is enough, twice is too much. The entrance grilles of the château de Villers have had curious fates. The first, which marked the way into the garden enclosed by a wall, was dismantled and melted down to make canons in the war of 1870. The second almost disappeared too, carried off by German soldiers in their retreat at the

Opposite:
The splendour of rhododendrons.

time of the Liberation. The inhabitants of the commune opposed this strongly and in the end the work which is seen today remained in place.

This is a little story, part of the big history, of a château and its park which figure among the jewels of the regional heritage. It was built in the 17th century on the site of a Roman villa, and these days the château is surrounded by a 50 acre park comprising two garden styles. One part, from the 17th century, is very strict with its great alley of beech trees, a main courtyard and borders surrounded by walls opening in a half-moon shape to the second part, which is an English-style garden.

The garden was fully designed in the 18th century, and is listed these days: you will find a planted ring for dancing. This is where the labourers from the château's farm used to come in earlier days to amuse themselves

to the sound of violins and to celebrate the end of the harvests. The local wine played no little part in creating the ambience: here until recently, as in other parts of Lower Normandy, vines were cultivated. The trees planted in the park come mainly from America. The arboretum is well known to specialists, a beautiful spot and a beautiful history.

Open from Easter to the end of September and upon reservation.

BEAUMESNIL (Eure-et-Loir): Madame's garden

This is a real beauty, a park designed by one the pupils of Le Nôtre, a magnificent 17th century château and superb pools which are a real pleasure for the eye. It is said to be the perfect prototype of the baroque style and the concept of the whole is a model of the type. The history of the spot originates from the time of the

The château of Villers-en-Ouche (Orne).

63

crusades. There remains a feudal moat from this era, which has been transformed into a maze. The 18th century garden has been changed many times, including the creation of an avenue of lime trees which still exists. Together with its maze and its pool, you must also see and walk through "Madame's garden", a delightful rose border.

Open from Easter to the end of September.

Cascade of wisteria on the Japanese bridge at Giverny.
(Photo Pierre Bérenger, "Normandy and its Gardens", Ouest-France publications, 1999).

GIVERNY (Eure-et-Loir): just like a picture

What can we say, which has not already been said, about the Giverny paradise? What can one say about the water lilies, the beautiful house and this garden which figures among the best known in the world? Giverny, Monet and his water lilies bring in a rush of tourists who queue up to visit the place. There is no end to the crowd of admirers. It is a work of art, a pure marvel of nature designed by the artist, his greatest work of art. Claude Monet had a passion for Giverny and its fine garden. First of all the painter rented the building which can be visited today, before buying it in 1880. He spent forty-three years here, composing the flower beds, marrying the colours according to the seasons, imagining new expanses around the "Norman close", from the water garden to the shade of the wisteria around the Japanese garden. It is always a real thrill to walk here, a lesson about life and flowers, a glimpse of the universe of the master of impressionism. Once you have visited the garden, you can also go into the house and see some of the rooms including the marvellous kitchen.

What else is there to say? Great specialists on Monet have studied the question, with details of each corner of greenery, each plot of land, each plantation. A single piece of advice: the best thing is to go there and look at it all, for the pleasure. For the pleasure alone...

Open from April 1st to November 1st every day except Mondays. Also open on Easter Monday and Whit Monday.

ARBORETUM D'HARCOURT (Eure-et-Loir): at the foot of the tree...

This is a unique model. It is a creation to try to acclimatise exotic plants. The Harcourt arboretum displays 400 different species of trees and bushes spread over 25 acres. It was created in 1802 and its collection of deciduous trees and conifers comes from all over

the world. You will find impressive sequoia here and "local" species grow side by side with exotic plants in perfect harmony. The Harcourt arboretum – the domain is the cradle of the great family from Normandy – figures among the most important domains of this type in France. For connoisseurs it is a reference and for others it is a pretty walk.

Open from March to June and from mid-September to mid-November every day except Tuesdays. Open every day from June 15th to September 13th.

Mosaic of spring colours.

Marriage of iris and phlox.
(Photo Pierre Bérenger,
"Normandy and its Gardens",
Ouest-France publications, 1999).

Angélique's gardens (Eure).

Water games in the Rouen Botanical Garden.

LE NEUFBOURG (Eure-et-Loir): flowers and music

Between Neufbourg and le Bec-Hellouin, the site is majestic and carefully organised. In the shadow of the 17th century château restored in the 18th, the park extends over some 18 acres and comprises borders, lawns, mazes and ornamentations. It was restored in detail following plans from the 17th and 18th centuries. The result corresponds to the hopes of the new owners who have turned it into a crossroads for meetings and entertainment. Seminars and concerts are organised here on a regular basis. The English-landscaped park includes some very fine and old trees.

Open from May 1st to September 15th every day. In March, April and from September 16th to November 30th, open at weekends.

ROUEN (Seine-Maritime): a breath of fresh air

A cool area in a town which sometimes needs it badly. A breath of fresh air is guaranteed and a delightful walk through this garden, formerly the Trianon park, also called the "Planterose" garden after one of its former owners. The park was bought in 1691 by Louis de Carel who designed the garden and had the pools built. These days, extending over 20 acres, it groups

together botanical collections which are references, both outside and inside greenhouses, combining a section which is "à la française" with a more relaxed and landscaped section with very fine trees. The garden is arranged around a 17th century pavilion, a

19th century orangery and greenhouses including the botanical pavilion and tropical greenhouses. It is a successful institution in Rouen: year in year out the botanical garden is visited by some 200,000 verdure enthusiasts.

Open every day.

MONTMAIN
(Seine-Maritime):
Angélique, the rose

A pretty name for a pretty garden. Gloria and Yves Le Bellegard christened this garden of old-fashioned roses with the name of their daughter, in her memory. For here, in Montmain, in the kingdom of Angélique, the rose predominates and perfumes everywhere with its delightful scent. The domain, overlooked by a fine manor from the 17th century which has been carefully restored, contains about 2,000 varieties of roses. A second garden was created in 1996, devoted to colours and composed of many perennials.

Open from May 1st to October 15th every day except Tuesdays.

VANDRIMARE
(Eure-et-Loir):
paradise on...earth

This domain belongs to very special gardeners, gardeners in their souls

and through their passion. Gilles and Marie-Christiane de La Conté have turned their family garden into a delightful walk. Here everything is simple and wonderful: the park comprises a succession of contemporary gardens which are said to ravish the

Left:
Rouen, the Botanical Garden.

Alley of roses at Montmain (Seine-Maritime).

The gardens and château of Vandrimare (Eure).

senses. Visitors can touch the plants, taste the fruits. The flowers, the plants, and the fruits are "arranged" by theme according to choice. First of all a border of perennials, then a garden for touching, a cloister garden, a berry garden, a shrub garden and the maze, not to mention the water garden. The owners call their domain a little "paradise" which they have only recently opened to visitors. This "paradise" is promised a beautiful future...

Open from April 1st to October 31st, from Friday to Monday and bank holidays.

LES FORRIÈRES DU BOSC (Seine-Maritime): geranium country

Never confuse geraniums with pelargoniums. If you would like to see the difference, take a tour of this fine domain devoted entirely to perennial geraniums, not to be taken for a pelargonium, the false-real geranium to be seen on balconies or on window-ledges. This garden is said to be the combination of an ornamental garden and a collector's soul. The gardeners, Doctor Evrard and his wife, are real enthusiasts who are known and recognised in their special field. They deal with nearly 500 different varieties of geraniums. A beautiful kingdom for a garden which combines types and colours. In all, there are more than 2,000 plant species presented perfectly simply and with great pleasure.

Open from May 15th to October 15th, on Thursdays, Saturdays, Sundays and bank holidays.

CLÈRES
(Seine-Maritime):
Joan's flowers

The spot is bursting with history. It is said that the château of the Jean-Delacour zoological park at Clères was built on the ruins of the castle where Joan of Arc spent her last night before her trial. The park is also full of memories: it was created in 1919 by the famous ornithologist Jean Delacour who wanted to shelter his numerous birds and animals here. The domain, spread over 162 acres, was opened to the public in 1930 and now belongs to the Natural History museum. There are 250 bird species living together around the Renaissance château: swans, geese, jays, cranes, peacocks, pheasants etc. In

The gardens of Vandrimare (Eure).

69

Bosmelet,
vegetable garden.

CLOS DU COUDRAY
(Seine-Maritime):
a micro-climate

Specialists say that there is a micro-climate here which plants love. As proof: here is a puzzle, a sort of bric-a-brac of gardens with 6,000 vegetal species. The Clos du Coudray, half way between Rouen and Dieppe, suits the rarest and most exotic of plants. Some can be seen which come from very far, such as China or South America. There is enough here to satisfy any neophyte, and to encourage any budding gardener. Varieties of holly, deciduous varieties, trees and shrubs are to be found side by side around a very pretty rose garden which can be admired in all seasons. Le Clos is 25 kilometres from the sea as the crow flies: sea spray is good for it.

Open from Thursdays to Mondays and bank holidays from April 11th to November 1st.

total about 1,800 birds enliven the 32 acres reserved for them. The park itself was designed for them with a lake, a river, rockeries and many plants. The spot also shelters antelopes, wallabies, and gibbons roaming half-free. Joan of Arc would certainly have liked it...

Open every day from March 15th to November 30th.

The château of Bosmelet
(Seine-Maritime).

AGAPANTHE
(Seine-Maritime):
there was a little garden...

Nestled in verdure, a story of enthusiasm and a little garden left by his parents and cultivated with care. This is Agapanthe and its history. Alexandre Thomas, landscape architect, took over the passion for this land inherited from his family. He created an intimate garden, with great taste, emphasising a succession of decorative plots. Each piece of greenery his its own and specific personality. You must take a walk through the sunken garden and then stop for tea to admire the spot. Bamboo leaves, flowery paths, box-tree borders: everything has been thought of to make you fall in love with the garden.

Open from April 15th to October 31st, from Fridays to Sundays and bank holidays.

BOSMELET
(Seine-Maritime):
sky colours
instead of rockets

Rainbows have replaced the V1 and the V2. This garden enclosed by walls has an amazing history: the German occupation almost annihilated all traces of it. Here, in this very spot, the German army installed the launching ramps for its famous rockets. The place was discovered by the Allies, was bombed and destroyed: nearly two hundred bombs crushed the property which almost never recovered.

These days, the colours of the rainbow are omnipresent: the vegetable garden was thus baptised to give homage to the colours of the sky. Laurence de Bosmelet, a persevering guardian, followed in the footsteps of her mother-in-law, former owner of the château destroyed by the bombing: she remodelled the spot, planted, replanted and gave the site its

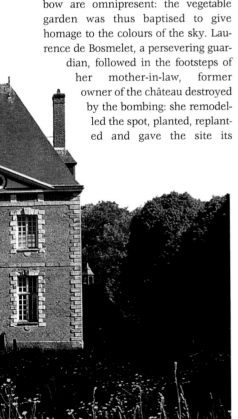

colour, colours which it no longer possessed. Her husband, specialist in Japanese, also went to work by creating an Asiatic kitchen garden grouping together some 500 Chinese cabbages. The rainbow kitchen garden, itself, holds 200 marrows, over 500 ornamental cabbages and 1,700 broccolis and cauliflowers, all surrounded by mixed borders of great taste.

Colours and scents mix well together here. Each plantation square is given the name of a precious stone or a rare material: sapphire, amber, garnet, ivory. This family garden, around the beautiful château which has been restored, is a diamond.

Open from May 1st to October 15th every day except Mondays and Tuesdays.

Garden entrance.

71

BELLEVUE (Seine-Maritime): beautiful roses

The château here is... a conservatory, as the mistress of the house says. "Everything is planned so that my plants live under the best conditions possible in order to bloom", recounts Martine Lemonnier who, together with her husband, runs the Bellevue domain at Beaumont-le-Hareng.

Hellebores are cultivated in the conservatory, the famous Christmas roses which are one of the leading specialities here. As its name indicates, the site offers

Meconopsis paniculata, originaire de l'est du Népal et de l'Assam, découvert par J. Hooker.
(Photo Pierre Bérenger, extrait de La Normandie des jardins, Éditions Ouest-France, 1999)

a very beautiful view. Too beautiful? The wind gusts and in order to protect themselves from unwanted regards and draughts they decided to hide the spot by planting trees first of all including some rare species from far away, like the famous white birch from China. The plants followed the trees, and the roses flowered in the conservatory. This is a story of logic and great elegance which visitors come from far away to admire.

The collection of Christmas roses has been noted in the botanical "Book of

Himalayan blue poppy
((Photo Pierre Bérenger, "Normandy and its Gardens", Ouest-France publications, 1999).

Records" and today serves as reference for the Conservatory of plant collections: it is the largest European collection of eastern hellebores. A beautiful view and… beautiful roses.

Open every day.

mune of Offranville put its money on the green. Jackpot!

Open from April to June and from mid-September to the beginning of October at weekends and bank holidays. Every day from June 1st to September 13th.

Christmas roses, orientalis hybrid, Bellevue. The plants of botanical origin are natives of northern Turkey and the Caucasus: discovered and introduced into France by J.-M. Pitton of Tournefort about 1700.
(Photo Pierre Bérenger, 'Normandy and its Gardens', Ouest-France publications, 1999).

OFFRANVILLE
(Seine-Maritime):
theme gardens

When a little commune decides to make a big garden… the story of the William-Farcy floral park in Offranville is exemplary. Exemplary because of the enthusiasm of the municipal gardeners who have taken the trouble to give this place one of the most beautiful flower borders of the whole region. It is not very big, but it is very beautiful.

The park is organised around a farm building from the 18th century and offers a rich and colourful circuit with a succession of a dozen theme gardens. There is a delightful mixture of roses and perennials for the pleasure of the eye and the walk. There is also a restaurant, a mini-golf, a camp-site and a horse-riding circuit. The little com-

Carefully lined up and bathed in light, the collection is accessible and each plant can be seen from all angles.
(Photo Pierre Bérenger, 'Normandy and its Gardens', Ouest-France publications, 1999).

MIROMESNIL
(Seine-Maritime):
big vegetables

*Thierry de Vogüe,
owner-gardener.*

"Red from Etampes" pumpkins.

The Saint-Saëns cabbage is the gardeners' gourmandise. Thierry de Vogüe, owner of the Miromesnil château, a fine building from the 17th century, the cradle of Maupassant, admits that he has a special weakness for big vegetables. The garden here is first and foremost useful, that is to say nourishing.

Thierry de Vogüe's parents planted them out of necessity, to provide the big weekend family meals and to cultivate what was simple and good. The tradition has been perpetuated with, in addition, a whole palette of colours owed, among others things, to the fine collections of clematis and flowerbeds of perennials, peonies, bell flowers. In the shadow of the forest, the only one like it – with its 3,500 trees - here is a garden with the scent of the dew at dawn and a delicious perfume of good things. Sit at table, Miromesnil is a real pleasure.

Open from May 1st to October 18th, every day except non-bank holiday Tuesdays.

VARENGEVILLE
(Seine-Maritime):
a family history

Varengeville is a family history. For four generations, they have cultivated, looked after, cosseted this land at the edge of

the sea, the Bois des Moutiers, unique in its category. When he bought the property in 1897, its creator, Guillaume Mallet, took his inspiration from the English parks of the Isle of Wight, helped by a young architect, Edwin Luytens, with whom the landscaper Gertrude Jekyll worked in the purest traditions of the "Arts and Crafts" movement, turning their backs on Victorian aesthetics. The gardens designed like this led to the immense park which in its turn led to the sea. The walk takes you through a succession of clearings, each marked by a predominant species: spectacular rhododendrons, azaleas, roses, hydrangeas... A white garden, an entrance garden, a magnolia orchard, a former kitchen garden transformed into a rose garden. Everything is laid out over more than 30 acres, which proves the extent of the work carried out by the Mallet family: a hundred years ago there was nothing here except a meadow...

Open from March 15th to November 15th, every day.

Rhododendron forest at Varengeville.

Moutiers wood.

75

The 1944 routes

"Promise, swear, die if I lie": they remember seeing the sky suddenly lit up that night. For a fraction of a second, no more. On the heights of the Val de Saire, to the north of Sainte-Mère-Eglise, the two neighbours looked again, over there at the tip of the coast: the night was coloured red by a flash of lightning. And then it all went black again, just as black as before. The two peasants by the sea still remember, many years later. They admit that, at the time, they never imagined for a moment that they were witnesses to the start of a great event, an extraordinary page in history. After all it was only a flare, just

another along the shore, a few miles from the Normandy coast. It was nearly 1 o'clock in the morning, perhaps a bit later, they are not quite sure now. But they are certain of one thing; they went back home to bed...

A few hours later, at 6.30 a.m. very precisely, on the side of la Madeleine, the beach of Sainte-Marie-du-Mont, the Americans came ashore. This was the send-off for an operation which was to enter the annals of Normandy's history for ever. D-Day was beginning. We are at dawn on June 6th 1944: the battle for the Liberation had just been launched. It lasted several months, from Utah Beach to Cham-

Left page:
***Normandy landings:
Omaha Beach – June 6th 1944 –
D-Day. American soldiers
leaving a landing craft
under fire from
German artillery.***
(© Arromanches museum)

***Normandy landings:
The engineers corps landed
first in the American sector
of Omaha: sheltering behind
defensive tetrahedrons***
(© Arromanches museum)

Normandy landings: June 6th 1944 – the artificial port of Arromanches: 1,250 acres able to handle 7,000 tons of equipment a day.

(© Arromanches museum)

bois, from the first days of June to the last days of August 1944: long weeks which here, on the edge of the sea, in the heart of the Bocage, are synonymous with incredible battles and terrible suffering. The two Normandy peasants from the Val de Saire were unaware of this when they went back to bed in their farms on the coast: they had been the first witnesses of an amazing story.

When the Allies were preparing their landing, they "cut" the sand into sections. They pointed at the map of Normandy to mark out five zones of attack from the sea: Sword Beach between Ouistreham and Lion-sur-Mer for the British 3rd infantry division, Juno Beach between Luc-sur-Mer and

Graye-sur-Mer for the Canadian 3rd infantry division; Gold Beach between Graye and Arromanches for the British 50th infantry division; Omaha Beach, between Colleville-sur-Mer and Vierville for the American 5th army corps and Utah Beach, around the bay of Veys for the American 7th army corps. These days, and since 1994, the date of the fiftieth anniversary of the Landings, the freedom beaches have become an integral part of a circuit "celebrating" the battle of Normandy. These are the 1944 routes.

OVERLORD

Bénouville, Bernières, Courseulles, Arromanches, Bayeux...

A bridge, a port and a press room!

This route follows the sea for most of the way, from Merville-Franceville to the outskirts of Caen, very close to Ouistreham, and as far as Bayeux. This is the story of Sword, June and Gold, the three beaches of the British sector. It is the story of a bridge which has remained famous, an artificial port with some traces still remaining at Arromanches, and the first reports written in an improvised press room, very close to the beaches.

It was just after midnight, that night of June 5th to 6th that everything began: the British paratroopers and commandos came in several hours ahead of the troops instructed to land in this sector. Their mission was clearly defined by General Richard Gale, in command of the 6th airborne division: to take the bridges over the river Orne to allow quick and rapid access to Caen in the rush of the imminent landings.

Three gliders, each with thirty men aboard, led by Major Howard started their approach: they landed in the night only a few yards from Bénouville bridge, slightly more than 6 miles from Caen. The bridge will remain famous for ever and, for history's sake, it is a great pity that it was

dismantled. But river traffic made this inevitable: fifty years after the landings it hindered the passage of ships taking the Orne canal, from Ouistreham to Caen.

"Pegasus Bridge", or what remains of it, on the footpath leading along the river, now canalised, is a rendez-vous which cannot be missed for those making the tour of the beaches and sites. Next to the footbridge there is a café which is just as famous: the Gondrée, named after its owner, has kept its original appearance. Veterans have made it a place of pilgrimage. Inside, carefully looked after, everything is in memory of the fabulous story of Major Howard and his men. The Gondrée café was certainly the first "bistro" to be liberated in France! However, it was only at 1.30 p.m. on June 6th 1944 that the reinforcements which had landed six hours ear-

Pegasus Bridge.

Major John Howard.

Stela on the beach of Colleville-Montgomery to the glory of the allied liberators.

Remains of German defences on Ouistreham beach.

same story from before the Landings. The little commune was liberated at 2.30 a.m. which made it, so they say, the first village to be liberated in France, even though Sainte-Mère-Église, in the Cotentin, also lays claim to the title. Next to the church, the British cemetery holds over 2,000 British tombstones, 323 German and 5 French. Here lies lieutenant Brotheridge, the first British soldier to fall, at the foot of Bénouville bridge. It was also at Ranville that General Gales, in command of the landing operation in the British sector, installed his command post: his bust now commemorates his memory on the little square which has been named after him.

Sword Beach stretches from Ouistreham to Lion-sur-Mer. Today it is an almost uninterrupted line of villas, some of which have an antiquated type of charm. The promenade is beautiful along the sea front, with old buildings and pretty beach huts on the strand. In Ouistreham, the Com-

lier on Sword Beach, crossed the famous bridge, object of all desires and all battles, to the sound of bagpipes.

The "piper", Bill Millin, has become one of the emblematic figures of this story: when crossing Bénouville bridge, ahead of the troops, he played "Blue bonnets over the border". The Ranville bridge is also part of the

mando museum illustrates the participation of the few French troops engaged in the landings battle, the famous Kieffer commando, named after the captain of corvette who led the marines. All around, the towns and villages are evidence of the assaults and combats: Colleville, Hermanville and its famous breach,

In remembrance of
Commander Kieffer.

Douvres-la-Délivrande and its German radar station, Saint-Aubin-sur-Mer and the remains of its old bunker, Bernières and the memory of the Canadian regiment of la Chaudière, Langrune-sur-Mer or yet again Luc-sur-Mer which marked the border between Sword Beach and Juno Beach, in the charge of British and Canadian troops.

The route follows this new portion of sand, from Saint-Aubin to Graye-sur-Mer. This is Juno Beach. Here the landing was late right from the beginning: the sea was too rough and prevented the Canadian and British troops from landing on time. It was only just before 8.00 a.m. that day of June 6th 1944 that the first soldiers set foot on the shore, on Vaux beach at Saint-Aubin-sur-Mer.

Between Fraye-sur-Mer and Courseulles,
the cross of Lorraine in memory
of General de Gaulle.

*Bernières-sur-Mer,
these days.*

*Arromanches:
the artificial port in 1944.*
(© *Arromanches museum*)

Not far from here, the little commune of Bernières-sur-Mer was liberated by the Chaudière regiment. In Montreal, the press anticipated the event on the morning of June 6th: "The Canadians will see Normandy again." This makes one think of the Dieppe disaster, two years earlier. The landing was not without its difficulties: the Allies were "greeted" by a hail of shelling. Ninety landing craft were destroyed here. The Beach Hotel at Bernières was the first press room for the war correspondents who sent their dispatches out over the whole world. Close by, inland, at Beny-Reviers, the Canadian cemetery holds the graves of more than 2,000 soldiers from the *"Belle Province"*, 335 killed on D-Day morning.

The landing at Courseulles was just as difficult. These days the commune is once again a pretty sea resort and an attractive fishing port. Together with its neighbour, Graye-sur-Mer, it commemorates an important event: here, at the border between the two villages, General de Gaulle landed on June 14th 1944 on his way to Bayeux. A cross of Lorraine has been erected here by the sea, in memory of this day. It was not easy to work out the exact spot to install it. The two communes both claimed paternity of the event. Finally, to keep everyone happy, the cross was placed at the precise border between the two resorts!

At Ver-sur-Mer, just next door, there is another cross of Lorraine, though more modest. Inscribed on the stela is an extract from the General's speech of June 18th 1940: "To all the

French: France may have lost a battle! But France has not lost the war!" Inland you can see the little commune of Creully. You have to go to the foot of Creullet castle, close by: this is where Montgomery installed his "canteen" from June 7th to 22nd 1944, a sort of caravan which acted as his headquarters. It was also at Creully that the BBC installed its aerials to transmit its reports back to London.

The coastline now becomes more tormented, and more rocky. You have to pass Asnelles, the landing site for Gold Beach – between Asnelles and Ver-sur-Mer more than 25,000 men came ashore in the morning of June 6th – to look down from the cliffs over one of the most well-known of the landing sites.

Arromanches-les-Bains will always remain famous because it was the scene of an incredible story. Here, at the foot of the dyke, the Allies installed their famous artificial port: between June 9th and 18th, some 115 coffers representing about 500,000 tons of cement were carried by sea

Visit to the Arromanches museum.

from England to protect the roadstead at this very point and to allow the passage of troops and equipment. Over 300,000 soldiers and 50,000 vehicles passed via Arromanches in the first days of the Liberation. In total, 2,500,000 soldiers and 4,000,000 tons of equipment transited through Arromanches.

These days you can still see several of the coffers which were used. In situ, the Landings Museum inaugurated in 1954 recounts this fabulous story. Next door, on the hill overlooking the spot, Arromanches 360 is ano-

Arromanches Museum

This exhibition, the only one of its kind in the world, on the very site of the event, is a messenger with a memory whose duty is to inform the younger generations of what happened here, in Normandy, on a certain June 6th 1944. Its animated models, its diorama and its film from the archives retrace the building and operation of the artificial port, which became the most important port in the world during the battle for Caen.

The famous Arromanches pontoons, formerly the artificial landing port.

De Gaulle at Bayeux in 1944.
(from "The Landings" by General Compagnon,
Ouest-France publications 2000)

ated France. On June 14th, two days after Eisenhower had stayed in the town, General de Gaulle installed the first members of the provisional government of the liberated territories. The town, liberated on June 7th at 10 a.m. by British troops, was spared the bombing all around. Two years later, the General returned to Bayeux to make his famous speech in which he set out the bases of the Vth Republic. Everywhere, including around the cathedral and the Queen Mathilde tapestry, the town recalls its memories from 1944. The Memorial Museum of the Battle of Normandy enters into details with its many documents from the archives, some of which are especially moving.

ther museum worth visiting: with a " cinema in the round" form it uses archives and present-day films to describe the era of the landings and the Battle of Normandy.

The famous batteries of Longues-sur-Mer are all around here. The site, overlooking the beach, is impressive. It is also unique: the German guns are still in place. The gunnery control is located in front of four pillboxes which can be visited. During the night of June 5th, the Longues batteries were the main target of the Allied bombers. In a few hours, 600 tons of bombs were dropped on this spot, and in the countryside all around you can still find the traces of this famous battle.

Further on you reach Port-en-Bessin, which was liberated on June 8th 1944 and then a few miles further, Bayeux, and the first steps of Liber-

D-DAY
Saint-Lô, Omaha, Colleville, La Pointe du Hoc, La Cambe, Saint-Clair-sur-Elle...

The longest day and civet of rabbit

First of all it was around the electricity power station, in the middle of the morning. Then a few hours later, around the station, in the middle of the afternoon. After 8.00 p.m. the bombardment was really under way. Jacqueline remembers it well: there was a civet of rabbit on the table and a fricassée of sand eels. Her town was one of the worst hit. Even today it is still said that it was the "capital of ruins" then. After the Liberation, there was a question of leaving it in that state, a mass of rubble, disembowelled houses, smoking ruins, to

The batteries of Longues-sur-Mer.

show the rest of the world the horrors of that night. The town could then have been closed in with barbed wire, a museum open to the skies and the nightmare of war.

Saint-Lô still bears traces of this terrible wound. The town has been rebuilt since: after the war it was only a shanty town. Over several years, a thousand wooden dwellings were built quickly to accommodate the refugees. Many of the inhabitants of Saint-Lô spent the night of the bombing in their town: they never imagined for a second that their homes could be the scene of such an attack and many had never thought of leaving to take refuge from the hundreds of bombs.

Right in the town centre, the ramparts hide a tunnel, which can still be seen, where hundreds of people hid during the following days and nights.

One witness recounts: "That night, the sky was suddenly filled with an enormous rumbling and then came

the cataclysm. All at once, the thunder fell on Saint-Lô with a catastrophic roar, with leaping flames. Growling, screaming, the incessant waves of planes attacked the town. It was red everywhere, black everywhere with acrid smoke, blood everywhere, dead everywhere in a mass of explosions, so many that it was impossible to tell one from the other. And this continued for hours..."

The D-Day route – the onslaught - goes past the prefectural town of the Manche, Saint-Lô, ravaged by the 1944 bombing. It then rejoins Bayeux via Utah Beach, the first beach conquered in the morning of June 6th and next the "bloody Omaha". D-Day, the longest day, ins-

Above:
End of July 1944: Saint-Lô in ruins after the bombing. It was taken by the US 29th I.D. on July 19th.
(from "The Landings" by General Compagnon, Ouest-France publications 2000)

Below:
Saint-Lô, Rue du Belle, close to the former prison.

85

The famous Pointe du Hoc.

*The devastated site
at the Pointe du Hoc.*

become a legend, and an emblem of D-Day.

Here, in this very spot, the landing of the Allied troops turned into a massacre. Commanding officer George A. Taylor, in charge of the 16th infantry regiment, said these terrible words only a few hours after the landing of the American troops on Omaha Beach: "There are two sorts of men remaining on the beach. The dead and those who are going to die." In less than three hours of fighting, the American army led here by General Bradley lost 3,000 soldiers!

The fighting was harder and fiercer than anywhere else. At 4.30 a.m. on June 6th 1944, nearly two hundred landing craft were launched about five miles from the beach. Approaching the shores, in rough seas, they were caught under a deluge of German shelling. Nearly one hundred German firing positions were deployed on the coast: the Allies were unaware of the fact that the German army had chosen this area to carry out its manoeuvres and double its forces! According to General Bradley: "On the beach, covered with wrecked boats, drowned vehicles and burnt out tanks, clusters of bodies lay soaked and deformed on the shingles just where they had fallen."

cribed for ever in the history of the Landings and the Battle of Normandy.

Along the circuit, there is a place dedicated to the memory of the dead: above the sea, overlooking this beach with its terrible memories, 9,386 soldiers rest in peace. The perfect alignment of the tombstones, the surroundings, the silence and the sea so close, make this American cemetery in Colleville an open air memorial. It reminds all those who come here to kneel, to lay down a flower, or to pray, the history of a stretch of sand close by which has

Slightly to the north, another sanctuary, another history. The Pointe de Hoc has remained the same as it was when the American soldiers decided to push on, convinced that there was a powerful German artillery here. Under a deluge of fire, the commandos of Colonel Rudder's rangers managed to climb the steep cliff just to discover, at the top, that the German batteries were no longer in operation: they had been moved further away only a few days before the landings! The site remains as it was. A granite arrow erected on the spot of the former firing position recalls the sacrifice: "the combatants rest here. In its chaos, the battle united them for eternity." Bodies of both American and German soldiers remain under the stones and the rubble. Out of the two hundred and twenty-five rangers who climbed the cliff, one hundred and thirty-five died.

Inland, on the road leading from Isigny-sur-Mer to Saint-Lô, the German cemetery at la Cambe is also a memory of those tragic days. Here 21,000 German soldiers lie. In the middle of the cemetery a granite cross marks the fact that two hundred and ninety six bodies of German soldiers were never identified.

The countryside all around saw terrible fighting. It was called the "war of the hedges". Lost corners of the Normandy bocage of woodlands and meadows, and special sites such as Saint-Clair-sur-Elle, Couvains, scenes of frightening and terrible combats. Between the bombardment of Saint-Lô and its liberation by Major Howie, a whole month passed! This tells the scale of the bitter fighting and the slow, very slow, progress of the troops of the American infantry. Everywhere, the villages here recount the same story and still bear the traces of the fighting. The little village of La Chapelle-Enjuger, just next to Saint-Lô, was the departure point of Operation Cobra, launched in mid-July 1944 by General Bradley: carpet bombing over several square miles which disfigured the landscape so much that even the inhabitants themselves, when they emerged from their refuges at the time of the Liberation, could not even recognise their own village!

Saint-Lô ranks among the towns martyred. Over 90% was destroyed. Only a few houses remained standing: there are some on the cliffs near Saint-Georges-Montcoq, which were spared by the bombs. Here, witnesses describe their town as a "huge shale quarry. No single home remained intact. Only the chimneys still pointing towards the sky were a reminder that here and there human beings had lived, loved, cried, suffered and died".

The longest day was also the blackest...

OBJECTIVE, A PORT

Sainte-Mère-Église, Utah Beach, Sainte-Marie-du-Mont, Crisbecq, Cherbourg...

Long live the young married!

The anecdote is well known: for Juliette and Georges, June 6th 1944 was to be a very special day. The two turtle doves, he a fanatic of cycling and she an apprentice hairdresser, had decided to exchange rings on this day. The two fiancés were all ready to celebrate their marriage in the little church of Sainte-Mère. But the paratroopers, with the imminent landings just a few miles away as the crow flies, from the hairdressing salon where Juliette worked, decided otherwise. The marriage in Sainte-Mère-Eglise, planned for June 6th 1944, was delayed for a few days and celebrated in a farm barn. The witnesses for the couple were American soldiers: the bride was beautiful, dressed in parachute silk.

We are here, on the route named "Objective, a port", a direct reference to the Allies landing on the

Juliet and Georges, on their wedding day in June 1944 in a garage in Sainte-Mère-Eglise transformed into a chapel. Juliette is wearing an American soldier's shoes.
(from 'Extraordinary stories about the longest day', by Philippe Bertin, Ouest-France publications, 1994).

Sainte-Mère-Eglise:
The memory of John Steele
is still alive.

Milestone 0,
departure point of
the Allied route
to liberate Normandy.

its surroundings: in images, it tells what D-Day was like here, through civilian and military witnesses.

The church of Sainte-Mère has become a sanctuary: in season, to please the tourists who crowd onto the square, they attach a model to the belfry, a replica of the famous John Steele, the soldier who "fell from the sky" during the night of June 5th to 6th and remained caught on the steeple. Taken as a target, he pretended to be dead for two long hours before, finally, being liberated! This story figures in one of the best-known scenes of "The Longest Day". Other scenes, other stories also made this little Normandy village famous, which claims loudly that it holds the title of the "first commune liberated in France".

The 82nd and 101st Airborne parachuted over Sainte-Mère-Eglise during the night of June 5th to 6th, at about 1.00 a.m. That night, the little village was fighting a fire, just next to the church square, where the thousands of paratroopers were to land. In total, 15,000 men were dropped over Saint-Mère and around. Many became bogged down in the marshes flooded by the Germans. There were many victims.

east coast of Cotentin on the morning of June 6th and taking Cherbourg. This was one of the special places of the Battle of Normandy. It is one of the best known as well, and passed on to posterity by a film which marked a whole generation. "The Longest Day", an American super-production, was filmed in Sainte-Mère-Eglise and

At Sainte-Mère, conquered by the troops in the middle of the night, a few hours before the landing at Sainte-Marie-du-Mont, the first military cemetery of the Battle of Normandy was created. Over 6,000 men rested here until 1948 when their tombs were transferred to Colleville-sur-Mer or they were repatriated to the United States. Among them, Brigadier General Roosevelt, cousin of the President of the United States.

The Airborne Troops museum whose roof, in the form of a dome, recalls the shape of a parachute, details this famous night. You may come across the curator of the museum in person, a veteran of the Landings who settled in Sainte-Mère-Église because in 1944 this is where he met the woman who was to become his wife! It was here, too, in Sainte-Mère-Eglise that they set up the first milestone marking the well-known "Liberty Route". The departure point, zero, corresponds to the route taken by the Allies to liberate Europe.

There is another milestone, with a double zero: this marks the first steps of the first soldiers on the beach of la Madeleine, only a few miles from here in the commune of Sainte-

Marie-du-Mont. Here too, they claim loud and long the title that they were the first to be liberated in France. This is partly true, since the first GIs landed here in Operation Overlord. A landing by error, since the site chosen by the Allies was not originally here but further north facing the dunes of Varreville. But the current and the wind decided otherwise: it is la Madeleine, called Utah Beach for ever, which history will remember.

Landing on Utah Beach,
June 6th 1944.
(from "The Landings" by General Compagnon, Ouest-France publications 2000)

Utah Beach

Utah Beach, the beach of
Sainte-Marie-du-Mont:
over 30,000 men landed
on June 6th morning.

The beach is immense and beautiful. On June 6th 1944, at 6.30 a.m., over 30,000 men and 3,500 vehicles came ashore here under the command of General Collins, in charge of the 7th army corps. The landing here was the least deadly of all, with two hundred killed. In the village of

D-Day at Utah Beach.

(from "The Landings" by General Compagnon, Ouest-France publications 2000)

Remains of an American amphibious vehicle nicknamed "Alligator".

Sainte-Marie-du-Mont, behind the famous beach, a "signposted" circuit recalls several facts and gestures of the first American soldiers. In the Sainte-Marie museum, the Landings Museum presents the chronology of the facts using many documents from the archives and a very careful museography. Here, you can see the dagger carried by a French pilot engaged in the Allied forces and who disappeared at sea, on the morning of June 6th 1944 while his plane was flying over the zone.

Ruins of the Crisbecq pillboxes.

There are villages, hamlets and "historic" sites all around Utah Beach, with their old German batteries such as those of Crisbecq, recounting the advance of the troops as far as Cherbourg. The North Cotentin port was of capital importance in the landings operation. Its deep-water dock allowed supplies to reach the troops. Cherbourg, after intense battles all around, was liberated on June 27th by the troops of General Collins. It took nearly three weeks, from Utah Beach or Sainte-Mère-Eglise, before the capital town of North Cotentin was finally returned to its inhabitants. Three weeks before the first Channel port could become the first "Liberty port" for ever.

THE CONFRONTATION

Tilly-sur-Seulles, Caen, Carpiquet, Aunay-sur-Odon, Vire...

In love with Tilly

Many years later, nearly fifty years after the Battle of Normandy, the former German lieutenant returned. During an entire Sunday, he tried to find the place, the farm, its owners and especially their daughter. He was told that they were all long since dead. All, except one. When he pushed open the door of the presbytery, tears came to his eyes. He had made the whole journey for her. And she, with her wrinkles and her back slightly bent, smiled at him tenderly. Were they very much in love fifty years before? In any case, they had never forgotten one another.

At Tilly-sur-Seules, the battle was fierce. It lasted eleven days, from June 8th to 19th. The commune, the gateway to the Bessin about 12 miles from Caen, was taken and retaken a good twenty times. The 30th British army corps suffered very heavy losses, as did the German defences, rich with one hundred and ninety tanks. Tilly did not resist: most of the commune was destroyed. Only the castle on the banks of the Seulles managed to conserve one of its wings. The little museum at Tilly describes the battle, the departure point of the operation named "Epsom". Nearby, the British cemetery shelters some 1,124 graves of soldiers and, a little further away, in the small commune of Chouains, another cemetery holds 46 tombstones including that of a soldier only 16 years old!

This is the departure point for the "confrontation", this circuit which is well worth its name: the Caen Memorial for Peace museum retraces the Battle of Normandy, but not only that. With its very careful museography, it tries to reflect on the events leading

Landing Museum at Utah Beach.

Left:
Site of Azzeville.

division, "fights" for peace in the whole world. It is true that the town which gave birth to it paid a heavy tribute to the history of the Battle of Normandy.

When they landed, the Allies wanted the capital of Lower Normandy to be one of the first towns liberated in the morning of June 6th. But it was not until much later – in mid-July – that British and Canadian soldiers finally entered the city where more than 30,000 Caennais were isolated. In the meantime, Caen had been pounded, bombed and flattened to a large extent. On July 7th 1944, 450 Lancaster and Halifax bombers dropped 2,500 bombs in less than one hour! The inhabitants had found refuges, including the cloister of the Abbaye-aux-Hommes. By mid-June there were almost 10,000 hiding there. Nearby, Saint-Etienne was sheltering almost 2,000 refugees at this period. The occupation troops, under Kurt Meyer, commander of the Panzergrenadier, were extremely cruel: on the morning of June 6th, the SS soldiers executed a large number of the detainees in the prison: their bodies were never found.

At Caen, the historic route of the Battle of Normandy takes in some of the best known sites: the Abbaye-d'Ardennes on the edge of the city, the airport of Carpiquet, Bretteville-l'Orgeuilleuse, Cheux, hill 112, a special place where there was a famous battle

Above:
Canadian and British troops entered Caen in mid-July 1944.
(from "The Landings" by General Compagnon, Ouest-France publications 2000)

Above right:
Caen, July 1944: Saint-Pierre church after the victory.
(from "The Landings" by General Compagnon, Ouest-France publications 2000)

up to wars and their train of great woes. The whole of the Second World War takes place under our eyes in a descent "into hell", a corridor leading down to rooms filled with many documents from the archives. The Caen Memorial for Peace, built on the place where a former command post once operated on a quarry which hid the support services of the 716th infantry

The Memorial for Peace Museum: halfway between history and memory.

or, again, Tilly-sur-Seules. The plain still carries traces of the fighting which led to the liberation of Caen on July 18th 1944. Further south, the town of Vire was also witness to the same endless fighting: it was liberated on August 7th 1944 after a ferocious

battle which destroyed everything in its path. A few miles from here, the little commune of Aunay-sur-Odon had the sad privilege of being, so they say, the most devastated in Normandy. Those in love with Tilly have never forgotten anything about this terrible confrontation.

COBRA, THE BREAKTHROUGH AND THE OUTCOME

La Chapelle-Enjuger, Périers, Coutances, Avranches, Saint-James, Mortain, Sourdeval, Flers, Alençon, Chambois...

A pocket of freedom...

"In the village, everything is in ruins, except for one house which still seems to be standing. There are only sections of walls. The church has lost its roof, the belfry has no top. The walls are very unsafe. The cemetery is terribly mutilated and the ground turned over. There are bodies which will have to buried a second time."

The priest of La Chapelle-Enjuger could hardly believe it: he could scarcely recognise the village which had been intact only two days previously. This is where Operation Cobra took on all its meaning and its tragic dimension: in less than two days, on July 25th and 26th 1944, nearly 20,000 bombs were dropped here over several hundred acres. "Carpet bombing" intended to make

Left:
The Memorial entrance hall.

93

The German cemetery at Marigny (Manche).

Tomb of a German soldier.

the link between Cherbourg and the south of the *département* of the Manche, to open up a passage so that the Liberation troops commanded by General Bradley could break through.

The circuit takes the route leading to the little village of La Chapelle, to the west of Saint-Lô. All the way, there are only rebuilt villages and hamlets; the war did not spare them. It was called the "war of the hedges", progress was so difficult in these corners of the Normandy bocage where each patch of land with its hedges represented a potential danger. Most of the town of Périers was destroyed, and two thirds of Coutances.

One man more than any other left his mark on the landscape: George Smith Patton, major general, led his troops as far as Avranches which was liberated on July 30th. Several communes around were also freed: Sartilly, La Haie-Pesnel, Gavray. This meant that the door to Brittany, close by, was open. After Saint-James where 4,410 American soldiers are

buried, Rennes was liberated a few days later.

Avranches remains faithful to Patton; a monument has been built at the entrance to the town in his memory: it was erected on the very spot where Patton stayed in the town. Very close, in the pretty bay enclosing the Mont-Saint-Michel, the little commune of Huisnes-sur-Mer holds a German ossuary where 10,000 German soldiers rest. You have to go further south to find Mortain, a special place for the Battle of Normandy. The town was the aim of the last German counter-attack in the *département* of the Manche. The civilians fled the intensity of the fighting and took refuge for long days in an abandoned mine. They went through hell: the bombing of the town lasted several days.

The historical area of the Battle of Normandy devotes several routes to this period around Mortain and Alençon. Sourdeval, between the two, is a special place to stop: several children from schools in Cherbourg found refuge in the old Labiche château. The building still exists. All along the circuit, at Flers, Tinchebray, traces of the Allied advance can be found, on the way to Alençon the first town in the Hexagon to be liberated by a French army. The Liberation Museum pays homage to General Leclerc who landed on Utah Beach in July at the head of his famous 2nd armoured division which liberated the town.

The encirclement, the route from Alençon to l'Aigle, allows visitors to understand the strategy used to encircle the German forces from the south, as they tried to retreat from Normandy. The outcome of the battle has a name: the famous Chambois "Pocket", the final combat for the Liberation of Normandy. Close by, Mont Ormel recalls the role played by the 1st Polish armoured division which came ashore at Arromanches and Courseulles on July 30th 1944. The town of Falaise was taken in the evening of August 16th. A few days later, on August 22nd, Poles and Americans succeeded in linking up at Chambois. Over 100,000 German soldiers were grouped here: the battle remains a terrible memory. More than 10,000 soldiers were killed and 50,000 taken prisoner. The others managed to flee under a hail of fire and a background of extreme desolation. A

memorial stands at Mont Ormel as a remembrance to these combatants. It retraces the history of the famous Pocket, which was going to open the route towards liberating Paris.

The Battle of Normandy had lasted nearly three months and claimed more than 600,000 victims among the combatants. The routes which visitors take today; from Cherbourg to Falaise, from Utah to Chambois, recount the extraordinary history and terrible suffering. Freedom re-found, at the price of so much misfortune...

The Battle of Normandy: in three months there were over 600,000 victims among the combatants.

British cemetery at Ranville (Manche).

The artists' route

Here, we enter the special soul of the land. Artists' houses – painters, writers, philosophers – fine manors, old shanties, gentle or rugged houses, everywhere the walls tell amazing stories. From the hamlet of Gruchy to Gréville-Hague, the countryside of Jean-François Millet, or to the château of Meromesnil, the birthplace of Maupassant, across the whole of Normandy, both Upper and Lower, the routes lead to landscapes where the artists lived. Here are a few, amongst many others...

Left page:
Villequier,
the Victor-Hugo museum,
on the banks of the Seine.

The Prévert house
at Omonville-la-Petite:
open to visitors.

OMONVILLE-LA-PETITE
Prévert:
Nénette's memories

The garden is small. A little house; the building somewhat squat and ill-proportioned. In the village of Omonville-la-Petite, over there at land's end, you might just have the luck to meet Nénette. She will tell you about Prévert and his house. On the first floor, the study-salon has remained intact, just as it was. The soul of the poet walks here, roving around. "When I

*The little village of Omonville,
by the Hague strands.*

come in here, I suddenly have the feeling that I have found him again. Just as if he had never really left the place", says Nénette, who was Jacques Prévert's daily help for nearly a quarter of a century. Sometimes, exhibitions on the ground floor of the house brighten up the surroundings.

Sometimes, when the wind is blowing outside, you can imagine what Prévert's last years were like. He and his wife Janine settled down here in 1971. The poet died six years later. His

wife continued living in the house until her death. The couple now lie in the little cemetery of Omonville, overlooking the sea. Next to them, there is another grave, that of Alexandre Trau-

ner the cinema designer. He introduced la Hague to Prévert. In the house, which these days is a museum, you will see a table right next to the window looking over the garden, and a few sketches hung there: they were drawn by Prévert. Little bits of paper, little drawings, little poems. This is where the poet's soul lives and Nénette's memories remain.

On the first floor of the Prévert house: the poet's study.

Left:
Alexandre Trauner rests just near his friend Prévert.

In the cemetery of Omonville-la-Petite.

Jean-François Millet.
"Gréville Church", 1871-1874.
Paris, Musée d'Orsay.
(from "Normandy,
the birthplace of Impressionism",
Ouest-France publications, 1999)

Opposite the Millet house,
this well became famous.

GRÉVILLE-HAGUE
Millet: Hague in his soul

Only a few years ago, nothing remained of the house where Jean-François Millet was born. It was just a pile of stones, a heap of rocks. Only the well remained standing on the other side, just as the artist knew it, the painter of peasants, whose "Angelus" was exhibited for the first time in 1865 and made him famous the world over.

Today the house lives again. In recent years it has been carefully and accurately restored. We are at Gruchy, a hamlet lost on the coast

of la Hague. Right in the middle, as the Norman poet Charles Frémine describes it, "an obscure alley, twisting, edged by cracked gables, all awry, everything covered with ivy". Here close to the village of Gréville-Hague, Jean-François Millet was born on October 4th 1814.

Gréville church.

At that time his family exploited 10 acres of land. He was the first child of a big family and the house where he was born was the main building, where his parents and his eight brothers and sisters lived. In the adjoining building, the ground floor acted as a cowshed and stable. Everything has been recreated here using furniture from that period: the renovators wanted to show what the interior of houses in Normandy were like at the time of Jean-François Millet. Upstairs, a "museum" of bric-a-brac humorously displays how the extensive work of the artist has been

used, to the point of putting some of his greatest paintings, including "The Gleaners", on Post Office calendars or Camembert boxes. If you would like to admire some of his real works, you must go on to Cherbourg. The Thomas-Henry museum has a fine collection, including a self-portrait.

The bust of Jean-François Millet, inaugurated in 1898, looks out over Gréville square. Next door is the little church whose magnificent "portrait" was painted so many times by the artist. He often painted la Hague and its surroundings: the hamlet of Gruchy, the Gréville cliffs, the Castel-Vendon rock, the Gruchy well, Vauville priory, the Landemer shores, the old house at Nacqueville or the Grimesnil farm at Equeurdreville. He died at the beginning of 1875 - on January 3rd – and lies in Chailly cemetery, near the grave of Théodore Rousseau. His memory remains in la Hague, at Gruchy...

Inside the Millet house, the "museum" of objects depicting works by the artist.

Gréville central square, dominated by the statue of Jean-Francois Millet.

SAINT-SAUVEUR-LE-VICOMTE
Barbey d'Aurevilly:
The dandy's frock coat

Jules Amédée Barbey d'Aurevilly rests at the foot of the castle at Saint-Sauveur-le-Vicomte. There is a tiny cemetery here, which can hardly be seen in the shadows of the ancient walls. Higher up, in the little town, is a house turned into a museum in memory of Jules Barbey d'Aurevilly. This is where he lived as a child, the house which belonged to his parents and, before that, to his grandfather on his mother's side, Hector Amédée Ango. He was born on November 2nd 1808 just next door, in the house of his great-uncle, the Chevalier de Montressel, during a "card game". A strange beginning for a man who never behaved like the others throughout his whole life.

The "dandy" of Saint-Laurent-le-Vicomte.

The manuscript of "Disjecta Membra".

He was called a dandy, and certainly was. His way of dressing is legendary: frock coat with pointed tails, waistcoats in red silk, white top hat and gloves, a gold-knobbed cane: the fashion figure was born. He never abandoned it, to the point that because of this some tend to forget what a productive and pleasing writer he was. It is often said that for a long time Barbey remained a writer who was "more famous than known".

The Barbey house at Saint-Sauveur-le-Vicomte is a lesson about the Aurevillien universe. By displaying many precious documents including the famous "Disjecta Membra", a manuscript of five hundred pages written in a variety of coloured inks and illustrated with sketches and arrows, the museum helps us to get to know and to understand better the author of "The Bewitched", "A Married Priest", "The Fiends" and "The Chevalier Des Touches". The famous frock coat can also be seen here, together with several personal

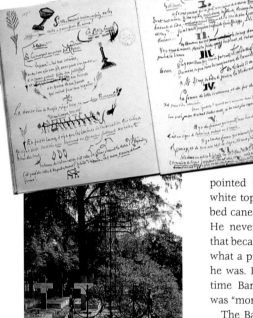

In the shade of the château of Saint-Laurent, the tomb of Barbey d'Aurevilly.

objects such as a moustache comb in blonde tortoiseshell, goose feather quills, an ink stand and a bottle of red ink. The whole is completed by a large iconography, paintings, drawings, engravings and photographs.

Canville-la-Rocque château, "theatre" for a Barbey novel.

The landscapes all around Saint-Sauveur belong first and foremost to Barbey: the heath of Rauville-la-Place, the minute cemetery of Taillepied, the Abbaye-Blanche at Nuefmesnil, Mont Etenclin near La Haye-du-Puits, the Olonde château at Canville-le-Rocque, the Carentan marshes and of course Valognes where he spent most of his summers. The dandy's frock coat and everything about him in the museum demonstrate clearly that this man, the "Walter Scott of Normandy", was definitely a writer unlike any other.

TOCQUEVILLE
Tocqueville: democracy
in Cotentin

This is not the château where he was born but played a part in his career. The family dwelling, on the East coast of Cotentin in the Val de Saire, very close to Barfleur, still houses his splendid, very splendid library. Alexis de Tocqueville left behind him a collection which is still a reference. "About Democracy in America" is the bible,

the history of an avant-garde vision. He was the first to point out the main lines of political and philosophical thought.

In the château, which he acquired in 1836, he wrote the greater part of his work, which in 1838 led him to membership of the Academy of Moral and Political Sciences and, three years later, to become a member of the French Academy. A successor in the constituency of Valognes from where he was elected member of parliament, founded the Alexis de Tocqueville prize which is awarded regularly for a work of political reflexion. Among the laureates, in no special order, Raymond Aron, Octavio Paz, François Furet and Louis Dumont can be cited. When he retired from politics – he was Minister of Foreign Affairs under Louis-Napoleon Bonaparte – Alexis de Tocqueville devoted the greater part of his time to writing a work which is yet another reference: "The Old Regime and the Revolution", which appeared in 1856. He was the first, before anyone else, to recommend the independence of justice and to fight for freedom of the press.

CAEN
Malherbe: closed house

There is no possibility of visiting the house of François de Malherbe. You can pass in front of it, in rue Saint-Pierre in the heart of Caen. It is a fine building whose facade has recently been restored with great care. The house itself is closed to the public, but all the surroundings are reminders of the poet who was ordered to write the *"vers galants"* love

Tocqueville's manor, on the east coast of Cotentin.

Rue Saint-Pierre at Caen, the fine Malherbe house after restoration.

poems for King Henri IV. There is a square named after him, the biggest lycée of the city, and a cinema in the centre of town, and even the footballers are called the "Malherbists"! "Come on, Malherbe, Come on, Malherbe", can be heard on Saturday evenings, as 8 o'clock chimes, chanted by the football fans. François de Malherbe could have written a poem about it, perhaps! He was born in Caen in 1555, and studied there before beginning his "career". He wrote one hundred and thirty-six poems inclu-

"Recherche du temps perdu". There is a subtle perfume, slightly antiquated, which provides all the charm of this resort which, in many ways, has managed to remain authentic, which is certainly not the case for many of its neighbours. Just a few incongruous residences at the end of the promenade have to be forgotten and you can plunge into the Proustian universe incarnated by the Grand Hotel. His parents introduced him to the place: between 1907 and 1914 he came here

The port of Honfleur: Here, Boudin and Satie have their "museums".

ding these words which are the best known "And rose she lived as the roses live, the length of a morning".

CABOURG
Proust: Marcel's room

The search takes you along the fourth floor of the Grand Hotel. The bedroom, a little room whose only opening is a small circular window, is said to remain as he knew it. Cabourg rhymes with Proust and vice versa. Here, along the front, facing the sea, behind the gardens of the fine casino, everything is reminiscent of the author of the

every summer, rarely going out and working hard. His room was his universe: he was happy to watch the sea alone, sheltered from the winds behind the big bay windows of the Grand Hotel salons. Do the same, never forgetting that at tea-time, the "must" here is to order... a madeleine cake.

HONFLEUR
Boudin, Satie: neighbours

In an old wooden house with a carriage gateway, in rue Saint-Léonard. In a beautiful wood-framed house in rue

Haute. The two men were neighbours when they were born, with several years between them. The first to be born, on July 12th 1824, was Eugène Boudin. The second was born in 1866. These days, Honfleur, their birthplace, pays homage to them and celebrates their memory without forgetting those who, like Alphonse Allais, also a native

din lived in Paris and at Deauville, although he stayed in Honfleur regularly between 1850 and 1859. Among the works reflecting his landscapes, the best known are the banks at Honfleur, the Saint-Siméon auberge, the pastures bordering the estuary and the Grâce coast. Three-quarters of these paintings are dated 1856-1859.

of Honfleur, made this little port their secret garden and their source of inspiration.

The Eugène-Boudin museum has collected several of the artist's canvases including a few famous portraits, an unusual genre in the universe of this painter. The artist left several of his works to the town of his birth, and this local son is said to have produced nearly 4,000 paintings and 7,000 drawings, including one hundred and twenty (only) devoted to Honfleur and its close surroundings. Once his career was established, Bou-

Satie is a completely different personality, another universe. It suffices to push open the door of one of "his" houses to see this at a glance. The composer built himself an unsettling world, surprising and somewhat provocative. It is said that he who invented music for films was a temperamental collector. In the Satie houses several of his objects can be found, each more peculiar than the next: a shoe violin, a trumpet with a bellows or a monkey automaton. The house museums of the welcoming inhabitants of Honfleur offer an introductory circuit to the composer's universe.

Eugène Boudin: "Honfleur Surroundings". About 1854-1857. Photo Gallery Schmit, Paris
(from "Normandy,
the birthplace of Impressionism",
Ouest-France publications, 1999)

The Vacquerie house, in memory of Léopoldine, Victor Hugo's daughter.

Picture painted by Victor Hugo when in exile in Jersey.
Private collection (from "Rennes", Ouest-France publications, 1997)

VILLEQUIER - CAUDEBEC-EN-CAUX
Victor Hugo:
in memory of Léopoldine

This bourgeois house is the one immortalised by Victor Hugo in *"Contemplations"*. It is also that of another memory: that of his cherished daughter Léopoldine who drowned in the river Seine in 1843 with her husband, Charles Vacquerie whose family owned the house which has become the museum of today.

The *département* of Seine-Maritime bought the house in memory of Victor Hugo and his family. The property dates from the first half of the 19th century. It was built by Aimable Vacquerie, an ocean-going captain who wanted to have a holiday residence. The Hugo family stayed there several times and Victor's daughter, Léopoldine, married Charles the ship owner's son on February 15th 1843. This house should have been a happy home; but seven months after their wedding the young couple drowned only five hundred yards from the property. Victor Hugo's sadness was immense, and several years later he wrote *"Contemplations"*, which appea-

red in 1856. Inside the Vacquerie house there are many original documents, sketches by Victor Hugo, sculptures, autographed letters, photographs and period furniture. This is a journey back in time of an especially moving nature.

CROISSET – CANTELEU
Flaubert: Emma's shadow...

Was Emma Bovary born here? It is very possible. Gustave Flaubert worked here endlessly, obstinately and

strictly. A hundred times, even a thousand times he threatened to throw away this "terrible and infernal" book he was writing. His memory is preserved at Croisset, very near Rouen. In 1844, a few months after the first nervous breakdown of his son, Gustave Flaubert bought this bourgeois house in Croisset; nothing remains of it except an 18th century pavilion standing on the edge of the property. The house, repurchased by the "Friends of Flaubert" in 1905, was donated to Rouen City, which turned it into a museum. There is a collection of thirty years of personal objects: a paper cutter with his monogram, a squat inkstand, goose feather quills, a Buddha on top of a display cabinet and several souvenirs of the writer. Next door, the Cantelou town hall holds his personal library of no less than 1,300 books.

Pavilion of the Croisset house: the memory of Flaubert.

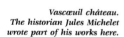

Pierre Corneille was born here.

been turned into a museum in memory of the writer, a theatre man who had his first big success in 1636 with *"Le Cid"*.

A few miles from Rouen, there is another building with other memories: Corneille's country house at Petit-Couronne, "the house in the fields" dating from the 16th century, preserves the memory of the Normandy writer and his family. Beginning with period furniture, an effort was made to try to recreate the atmosphere of bourgeois life in the country, from Henri IV to Louis XIV. The *"Imitation de Jésus-Christ"* is on display here, corrected by the hand of Corneille, as well as several original editions of his works. There are engravings and sculptures, and documents from the archives to complete the "museography". All of this is situated in surroundings which are perfectly adapted: in 1944, a 17th century kitchen garden was created.

ROUEN
Corneille: triumph without glory...

"Le Cid" was born in Magpie Street. The house, an old traditional building in the centre of town, typical of the Rouen region of the 17th century, is still standing: Pierre Corneille was born there and lived there until 1662. It is said that most of his major works were created here. The house was restored at the beginning of the 20th century, and has

VASCŒUIL
Michelet: history of France

Vascœuil is a unique place for meditation. After travelling across Normandy up and down and to and fro, from Granville to Dieppe, Jules Michelet decided to settle in the beautiful château of Vascœul which he discovered in 1841. He

Vascœuil château.
The historian Jules Michelet
wrote part of his works here.

The family house of Jean de La Varende at Bonneville.

organised his study there and over a period of twenty years wrote most of his works including his famous *"Journal". "L'Histoire de France"*, an immortal work, was written in the Vascœul château whose name is now associated with the historian for ever. It is a casket of verdure and a superb property, which has become a site listed by the Historical Monuments. It is the only Michelet museum in France and, at the top of the tower, his study has been recreated while numerous mosaics and sculptures "ornament" the park *à la française*.

LE CHAMBLAC – BONNEVILLE
Jean de La Varende
Norman through and through

Jean de la Varende, Norman to his very finger tips, was a "regionalist" in his soul. Most of his writings - fourteen novels and eleven collections of short stories – refer to the land where he saw the light of day. He was born in Bonneville in the family property which he hardly ever left. These days it is still private property, but nonetheless it is possible to visit the study of the author of the famous *"Nez de Cuir"* or *"Cadoudal"* and to discover a fine collection of his model boats. He made more than two hundred. After his books and writings about Normandy, this was his second great passion. He was made a member of the Goncourt (author's prize) jury in 1942 and left three years later, signing his letters after that by "Jean de La Varende, non-Goncourt". Bonneville château is all his own work: he created a little garden *à la française* with his own hands, featuring box hedges trimmed in the shape of a chess game.

VARENGEVILLE
Braque: up there on the cliff

Varengeville is not far from Dieppe and Tréport. There is a cliff near Varengeville. And on this cliff there is a church. And at the foot of this church there is a sailors' cemetery overlooking the seas. Georges Braque remains the emblematic figure of the site, one of the most beautiful on the Alabaster Coast. The painter took refuge here, to such an extent that he installed his studio and built his house. He was not the only one to fall under the charm of this little village in Normandy. Others, like Corot, Renoir, Monet, Pissarro or Miro made it their favourite place, the secret garden for their works. The little church of Varengeville has a stained glass window signed by Braque, whose tomb in the sailors' cemetery is marked by the famous dove.

MIROMESNIL
Maupassant:
The roots of *Bel Ami*

"I love this country because my roots are here": Maupassant talking about Miromesnil, his family cradle.

Bust of Maupassant.

His roots are here and nowhere else. Guy de Maupassant is the man of a land where everything is a reminder of him. Rouen, Dieppe, Yvetot, Granville-Ymauville, Etretat… and of course Miromesnil his family home. The sites, places, landscapes, little villages and narrow streets belong to him. He wrote magnificent pages about them, amazing stories. "I love this land and I love to live here because my roots are here, these deep and fragile roots which attach man to the earth and where his ancestors were born and died…", wrote the author of *"Bel Ami".*

The château of Miromesnil is the emblematic spot, the memory of a family life. Guy de Maupassant was born here on August 5th 1850. The park with its centuries-old trees is magnificent and the interior of the Louis XIII house displays, among other things, the birth certificate of the writer. There are also traces of the author at Oherville, in the Auffray manor which has become the International Guy de Maupassant Centre, and also at Etretat, in the shade of the "Guillette", his house in Normandy. He knew the landscapes of the Caux country by heart, to such an extent that he acted as guide for Flaubert who was preparing his *"Bouvard et Pécuchet".* He knew the area so well that memories of the splendid storyteller can be found almost everywhere here, around Gonneville or Etretat.

GIVERNY
Monet: the master's eye

The house is known throughout the world. In season, crowds rush there and queue to discover or rediscover the wonderful garden with its water lilies. Some say that this corner of verdure at the foot of the building, the work of the artist, is his greatest work. The house is also well worth the visit. There are several rooms and several

The world of Monet, Giverny garden with its thousand colours.

objects which recall the painter of the "Water-lilies". The reading room, the bedroom with his bed and the roll-top desk, the workshop salon, the dining room and the wonderful kitchen. Everything here tells about the master who inhabited the little village at the boundaries of the Ile-de-France between 1883 and 1926. He is buried here. If you wish to understand Monet, or to rediscover him... you must go to see the universe where he belonged. A world of colours, full of infinite grace which makes the site exceptional and very special. The walk in the garden and the visit of the house are wonderful moments... to savour for the pleasure of the eyes...

The sailors' cemetery of Varengeville, dear to the heart of Georges Braque.

Claude Monet: "Women in the garden", 1867. Paris, Musée d'Orsay.
Photo R.M.N. (from 'Normandy, the birthplace of Impressionism', Ouest-France publications, 1999)

The local flavours route

Eat and drink!

Oysters from the open sea with a glass of "calva", Normandy is rich in these products which are the delight of gourmets. At table!

Ciders from the Auge country

This is the "must", the absolute reference. However, there are as many local ciders as there are hedges in the Normandy bocage but whatever others may pretend, this is the reference. Since 1996, cider from the "pays d'Auge" has been awarded the label of guaranteed origin vintage. In other words, it is cosseted, looked after and above all, controlled. It was really developed from the 16th century, although it had existed long before that. At the time, the kings of France tried it and adopted it. To your good health!

SCÈNES DE LA VIE NORMANDE
25. Visite à la Ferme
Mesurage des pommes.

Measuring the apple crop.
(Monique Sclaresky collection)

Above left:
Good cider from M. and Mme Joui at Irai (Orne).

Left page:
Apple trees in flower.

The apple and cider route

A very small trip – hardly more than twenty-five miles – between Caux country and the Bray country. The circuit takes the valleys of the Scie and the Varenne with their happy landscapes, old apple trees, cultivated orchards and modern cider-works. To be discovered near Auffray and Longueville-sur-Scie in Seine-Maritime.

The cider route

In Calvados, the Auge country has a high reputation among enthusiasts of champagne cider. The cider route was created by the producers' union of the "Cambremer vintage". It groups together about thirty producers who offer ciders with the guaranteed origin label. On the way, stop for a while in the little village of Beuvron-sur-Auge, which is worthy of a postcard.

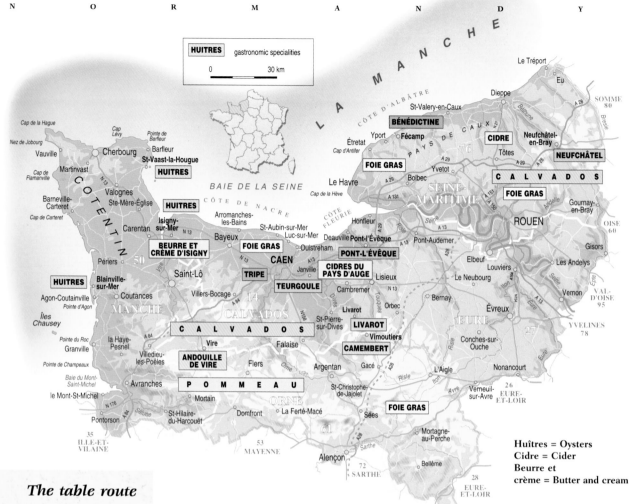

HUÎTRES gastronomic specialities
0　　　30 km

Huîtres = Oysters
Cidre = Cider
Beurre et
crème = Butter and cream

The table route

It deserves its name because it concerns gastronomy. In the Manche, many producers, often farmers, have grouped together to offer this itinerary dedicated to the land and its quality products. The route follows several top gourmet stops: Lessay, for its "Cotentin hams", Saint-Sauveur-Lendelin for its foie gras, La Baleine for its smoked andouille, Brecey for its honey. Other places are marked on the circuit, which also includes several local specialities such as the coppersmiths in Villedieu or the faiences of Mont-Saint-Michel bay.

Open-sea oysters are "bred" on the west coast of Cotentin.

114

Normandy oysters

Those who talk of oysters often talk about Marennes or Cancale. This is unfair to Normandy since it has very old high quality oyster culture basins around its coasts, for example at Saint-Vaast-la-Hougue on the east coast of Cotentin. Like the cider, the oyster has its vintages and its specialists who can tell the difference by tasting. They will tell you that this one has a pronounced

flavour of hazel nuts while another is much more iodized. Depending on individual taste, you can choose between the oysters from Isigny, Saint-Vaast or Blainville. We prefer the latter, but it is an entirely subjective matter: on the west coast of Cotentin, the oysters are grown in the open sea in an area with the biggest tides in Europe.

Calvados

It goes without saying that this is to be consumed with great moderation. "Calva" deserves this, and should be tasted and appreciated as a rare product. It comes from strictly defined geographical areas and is usually compo-

Oysters parks
of Saint-Vaast-la-Hougue.

fashion? Never mind, a good calva cures all worries and, so they say, helps the digestion.

Camembert

Since 1983 this cheese has the guaranteed origin label and is to Normandy what the Eiffel Tower is to Paris, a monument known throughout the world, which owes its creation to Marie Harel, in 1791. Often imitated, but never equalled, camembert made out of untreated milk and moulded with a ladle is a real marvel. In order to respect its AOC label of guaranteed origin, a real camembert must be made from untreated milk which is not heated above 37°C. It contains 45% fat per 100 grams of dry extract. Do you like it ripe?

sed of brandy of different ages and from different local soils. This is why it is rare and why its high quality is appreciated by connoisseurs. Is the "Normandy hole" (a "digestive sip" in the middle of a heavy meal) still in

Monsieur Huet tastes his
"calva" at Cambremer
(Calvados).

Réaux Camembert,
moulded with a ladle.

The Camembert route

In Marie Harel country, the camembert is king. This circuit, 35 miles long around Vimoutiers, is entirely devoted to this cheese. The route follows the Auge valley, a green countryside with fine apple trees. Obviously, there is a stop in the small village of Camembert, the home town of the famous cheese with its fermented paste. This is a pilgrimage for all those who cannot resist a ripe and "runny" camembert...

20. La Vie Normande — Laitière à Ane

Milkmaid on a donkey.
(Monique Sclaresky collection)

was especially appreciated at the end the 19th century. This divine cheese is matured for at least three weeks. After that, it is a real treat!

Neufchâtel

This is the oldest of Normandy cheeses, a native of Bray country. It can be found in several forms: heart-shaped, a big heart, double blonde, square, a little brick... To each his special shape and its savours: maturing and salting vary according to the profiles of the cheese, which obtained its label of guaranteed origin in 1977.

Mme Brianchon producing cheeses at Neufchatel-en-Bray.

Butter and cream from Isigny

Butter, cream... and beautiful pastures. The decor is almost perfect: it is real Normandy, and the products from Isigny received the AOC label of guaranteed origin in 1986. A reference of quality for these milk products from Normandy's cows.

Livarot cheese.

Livarot

It is named after its village. In Livarot, in Calvados, they make... It was the brother of Pierre Corneille who noticed it in 1708 and specialists say that it is a cheese of character with a soft and washed paste. Its crust is encircled by ribbons, three or five, which is why it has been nicknamed the "colonel". It

Pont-l'Évêque

It is said that the monks in the abbeys of Normandy were the first to produce this delicious cheese. These days it is made from milk coming

Isigny-sur-Mer: the wash place.
(Monique Sclaresky collection)

from Normandy and from Mayenne. It is a cheese with a special character and taste, and received its AOC label of guaranteed origin in 1976.

Pommeau

Little by little, this alcohol from Normandy is making its mark. "The General", the trotting horse who won the America Prize at the end of January 2000, at the Paris-Vincenne racecourse, certainly gave its name a boost. The horse's owners thought first of all of calling him Général du Terroir but finally opted for Pommeau, in homage to the brew! Well done: the little horse, Général du Pommeau, reared in Saint-James in the *département* of the Manche, beat all the records and introduced the whole world to this aperitif 100% from Normandy. It is produced from a basis of cider-apple juice and calvados, and since 1991 pommeau has carried the guaranteed origin label. There are ninety producers scattered throughout Normandy – Manche, Calvados, Orne, Eure and Seine-Maritime – making nearly 800,000 bottles a year. Their orchards contain only cider apples with at least 70% "bitter" or "bitter-sweet" varieties. About thirty varieties of cider apples have been selected for the production of Normandy pommeau. Several weeks pass by between the apple harvest in October and November and the pommeau production, and then the alcohol is aged in oak barrels for nearly eighteen months. Pommeau is usually drunk as an aperitif, served cold. It can be recognised from its red amber colour with a pronounced aromatic bouquet.

Left:
Local products from Normandy.
(from "Best recipes with cider", Ouest-France publications, 1996)

Above:
Collecting cider apples.
(Monique Sclaresky collection)

The Neufchâtel cheese route

The Neufchâtel comes from the Bray country, between Neufchâtel-en-Bray and Forges-les-Eaux. This is a defined area for production and maturing: the circuit explains the production methods and the know-how of the cheese makers. This farm cheese, a real delight, is produced in six shapes: the little brick, the square, the blonde and the half-blonde, the famous heart and the big heart. Do enjoy it!

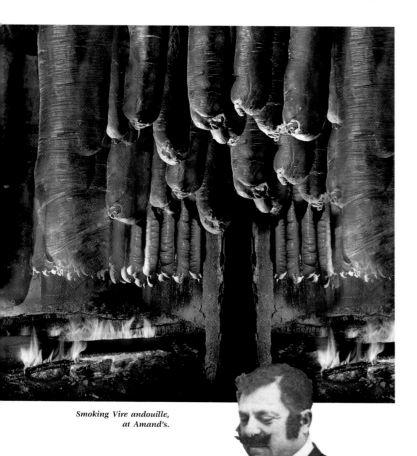

Smoking Vire andouille,
at Amand's.

Andouille from Vire

This great speciality from Vire needs no introduction: the andouille is the trademark of the town, its coat of arms, its badge. In the 18th century it was already part of the gastronomic heritage of this town among the woodlands and pastures of the Normandy bocage. The speciality is prepared using the digestive system of the pig and then smoked for six to eight weeks. The andouille sausage is then dipped, tied up with string and cooked in water for three to four hours. This fetish product of the Virois, and their great pride, is also a whole history of tradition and real know-how handed down from generation to generation.

Benedictine

A liqueur like this is worth any journey. It takes no fewer than twenty-seven plants and spices from the four corners of the earth to compose this precious Normandy brew: cloves from Zanzibar, vanilla from Madagascar, tea from Sri Lanka, myrrh from Saudi Arabia, saffron from Greece... all topped with vanilla pods and

Genuine andouille from Asselot & Son.

Left:
Andouille from Vire.
(Monique Sclaresky collection)

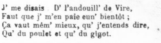

J' me disais : D' l'andouill' de Vire,
Faut que j' m'en paie eun' bientôt ;
Ça vaut mêm' mieux, qu' j'entends dire,
Qu' du poulet et qu' du gigot.

L'andouill' fait bien dans l' ménage,
Son effet est merveilleux ;
Y paraît qu' ça l'avantage
D' rendre l'homm' plus amoureux !...

Moi qui viens d' prendre eun' jeun' femme,
Et l'aim' du fin fond du cœur,
D' dix dégrés croîtra ma flamme...
Pour un mari, quel honneur !...

À BLACHER

lemon rinds and aged in oak tuns for at least a year. Benedictine is to Fécamp what the andouille is to Vire: a gastronomic institution coupled with a fascinating history. The product was invented in 1510 by a Benedictine monk from Fécamp abbey, dom Bernardo Vincelli. It was adapted to contemporary taste in 1863 by

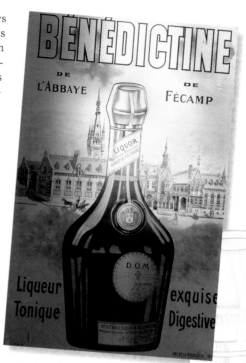

a wine merchant named Alexandre Le Grand, who gave the liqueur its renown and made it a local speciality

of the town. These days you can visit the famous Benedictine palace rich in its dozen stills in red copper and its superb cellars with enormous oak barrels where the precious mixtures rest. The liqueur from Normandy has become international: 95% of the production is exported, in particular to the United States, Europe and South East Asia.

Foie gras

Foie gras can also come from... Normandy! Since 1989, there has been an association of foie gras producers on the two banks of the Seine in Upper and Lower Normandy. The "Fermiers des Becs" group together forty-six producers who adhere to a quality charter and have regular visits to their premises. Normandy is the third biggest producer region for foie gras in France. It is a liver of high quality and benefits from a selected terrain: since a goose consumes up to 900 grams of grass a day, the Normandy bocage provides the best there is in this matter. Production has been increasing regularly recently with a multiplication of markets for Normandy foie gras in many towns in the region. They can be found in the spring and autumn in Valognes, Vire, Bayeux, Caen, Lisieux, Gacé, Alençon, L'Aigle, Bernay, Honfleur, Le Neufbourg, Rouen, Yvetot, and Le Havre.

*The abbey
of Benedictine
at Fécamp.*

The ivory and spices route

The circuit is restricted to Dieppe and Fécamp. Beginning in the Renaissance, Dieppe imported ivory which was carved here. Some of these very fine items are now conserved and presented in the town castle museum. As for the spices, they take the route to Fécamp, famous for its Benedictine. The palace-museum, devoted to the liqueur, recalls the astonishing and ancestral history of this divine beverage.

Teurgoule

People say that an old expression in the local Norman dialect gave this name to the recipe handed down over the generations. Teurgoule means "to twist the mouth" and implies that this dish, which used to prepared on the farms, was served as a boiling dessert when winter was at its coldest. Taken straight from the oven, where it had been cooking for at least five hours, they sometimes burned their tongues so much that they twisted their "goule" or mouth in a grimace. These days the delicious mixture, typical of Normandy, of rice, milk, sugar and cinnamon has been widely recognised. At Janville, on the edge of Caen, Alain Urban has made it his speciality: he produces about 2,000 bowls of teurgoule per day which end up on the shelves of the supermarkets. Janville has become the capital of teurgoule, a family recipe which bakers have cooked for ages in their ovens: in fact in needs long and careful cooking at over 100°C to succeed. Teurgoule has its faithful followers: a brotherhood of teurgoule gourmets in Normandy takes care of promoting it all year round.

Tripe

Every year, the city of Caen has a tripe festival. The recipe *"à la mode de Caen"* has become an institution, a fixed rendezvous which draws in the crowds and the gourmets. The origin

Alain Urban, the "pope" of teurgoule.

Mother's teurgoule.
(from "Aunt Jeanne's recipes" Ouest-France publications)

Fierville or teurgoule terrine.
(from "Normandy Desserts", Ouest-France publications, 1997)

La teurgoule de maman

3 litres de lait entier cru,
150 g de riz rond,
15 morceaux de sucre,
1 grand bâton de vanille.

Verser le lait dans un poêlon en terre (il ne doit pas dépasser les 2/3 du poêlon).
Ajouter le riz, le sucre et la vanille, et mettre au four. Le riz doit cuire très doucement pendant 3 à 4 heures. Il peut frémir mais il ne doit pas bouillir.

La teurgoule est le dessert normand traditionnel.
Dans ma famille, personne ne met de cannelle dans la teurgoule contrairement à certaines recettes, on préfère la parfumer avec un bâton de vanille.
Mais il y a malgré tout deux écoles en ce qui concerne la technique de cuisson :

Il y a ceux qui crèvent plusieurs fois pendant la cuisson la croûte qui se forme à la surface du plat, ce qui colore le riz et fait épaissir la peau.

Il y a ceux qui ne touchent à rien pendant 3 heures, estimant que le riz est plus crémeux ainsi.

Question de goût...

of the famous "tripe prepared the Caen way" is lost in the mists of time. There are said to be references to it from the 13th century. The recipe is attributed to the monk Sidoine Benoît, former cook at the Men's Abbey in Caen, where it was first accepted. The "tasty" dish then made

*At Ruault, the great specialist
of tripe "the Caen way".*

The wine route

This is a long and beautiful story. In the past, the Normandy vines were highly considered and several traces still remain. Enthusiasts, historians or oenophiles, still carefully cultivate the vine legacy, and three major districts can be mentioned: the vines of the Saint-Pierre vale by Mont-Saint-Michel bay, those of Argences close to Caen and, finally, those of Longueville on the banks of the river Seine. In the past, the monasteries played an essential part in encouraging the development of vines in Normandy. In times past, it was normal to bless the new wine in the churches. During the era of the Dukes of Normandy the wine from Argences – a white wine – was very popular and was drunk without moderation. References to its prosperity can be found: from the 11th to the 13th century the domain of the Ouézy Priory in the Argences district provided about 25,000 litres for Jumièges Abbey. These days, traces of the Normandy vine are maintained by the CEPVIN, the Centre for studies and promotion of historical Normandy vines, based at Cesny-aux-Vignes. Moreover, the little village has set the example: about a hundred vines have been planted around its church. For the anecdote, recently, during renovation, three small barrels of white wine from Cesny-aux-Vignes were discovered in the bell-tower of Bretteville-le-Rabet. There is also evidence of experimental vines in Thury-Harcourt, in "Swiss Normandy". Finally, a "local wine from Calvados" has been produced recently in Grisy, a commune close to Caen; there are 1,760 vine plants of different varieties which produce a "fruity and aromatic" white wine.

the round of the abbeys of France to end up later, and still to this day, on household tables. The "Tripière d'Or", a well known and enthusiastic brotherhood, has promoted the product as far as possible since 1952. Each year it organises the competition to choose the "best tripe in the world". There are a few rules which have to be followed exactly to make good tripe the Caen way: the different pieces must be cut into squares all about 6 to 7 centimetres on each side, it is indispensable to add a calf's foot, and the cooking must be slow, about ten to twelve hours!

INFORMATION ON LOCAL PRODUCTS

• *Normandy Food Processing Expansion Committee, Caen. Tel: +33 (0)2 31 47 22 47.*

• *Normandy Regional Institute for Food Processing Quality, Caen. Tel: +33 (0)2 31 47 22 52.*

The nets are ready.

Other routes, other stories...

Normandy is criss-crossed by these tourist and theme circuits which open up all the charm of the region, on the two banks of the river Seine. From the Perche, in the Orne, to the coasts of the Manche in Caux country, here are a few ideas for itineraries marked out by the Regional Committee for Tourism.

Pigeon-houses in Caux

These are witnesses of an earlier life, an epoch which has passed. The pigeon houses were usually built inside farmyards. The route takes you along the valleys of the Durdent, Valmont and Ganzeville and crosses the countryside of Caux.

The land of Emma Bovary

This circuit, in memory of Flaubert, comprises fifteen stops over about forty miles, east of Rouen. Leave from the promenade at Ry to discover on your way the valleys of the Crevon, the Héronchelles and the Andelle.

Sandstone circuit

Fifteen communes can be seen on this route, which takes you on a twenty mile trip around Saint-Valéry-en-Caux. Homage to sandstone and memory of the heritage of the buildings of this region including many castles, calvaries, churches and manors.

Médavy château. This isolated tower, topped by a dome with a lantern turret, recalls the existence of a previous fortified enclosure.

Left page:
Figurhead ornamenting the main gate of the Haras du Pin stud.

Studs and châteaux of the Orne

The Saint-Lô stud: in season, each week, tandem teams parade in the main courtyard.

The Haras du Pin is a marvel, a reference. It is one of the two national studs in Lower Normandy; the other is at Saint-Lô. The route around Le Pin includes the main historical monuments of the *département* of the Orne. You go through Domfront, Bagnoles-de-l'Orne, Flers, Sées, Argentan, Carrouges. This is a trip of 125 miles to discover castles and châteaux, manors, churches, studs, farms and listed sites.

Raymond Pitrey, in charge of the teams at the Saint-Lô stud.

Routes in the Perche

There are several itineraries marked out to discover the charms of this special region: forests and abbeys, châteaux and castles, pools, valleys and lakes, manors and traditions, sites and panoramas. In short, there is plenty to fill the itinerary, or even several: Mortagne (famous, among other things, for its "boudin" sausage), Tourouvre, Bretoncelles, Rémalard, Villeray, La Chapelle – Montligeon, Bellême (a magnificent forest) or Soligny-la-Trappe where there is a superb abbey...

The Haras du Pin,
a marvel of the horse world.

Below left:
A sober building from the end of the 17th century, Médavy (Orne).

Below right:
Dating from the beginning of the 16th century,
The Château du Repas at Chénedouit (Orne).

*Medieval fortress
at Pirou (Manche).*

*The majestuous
Beaumont house, from 1770.*

The landscape is not mountainous but is still very undulating north of the Orne. There are good walks here or you can take your car to the fine Grimboscq forest, by the Sainte-Anne chapel, or to Thury-Harcourt, Condé-sur-Noireau, Clécy, Flers, Pont d'Ouilly, Putanges, Ecouché. A piece of advice for those who like dancing to the accordion: on the way, near Coudray bridge, between Thury-Harcourt and Caen, you can stop for a while at the café where lovers dance on Sundays...

The eleven-sided tower of Bricquebec château.

From the Cotentin to Mont-Saint-Michel

This is the route of those who built Normandy. It takes in several of the most beautiful sites relating the history of the *département* of the Manche: Tourlaville château, known because it sheltered the tragic love of the Ravalets, the isle of Tatihou and its Vauban tower, Valognes and its fine Beamont house, Saint-Sauveur-le-Vicomte and its Barbey museum, Crosville-sur-Douves just nearby and its restored château, Bricquebec and its keep, Barneville-Carteret and its famous cape, Pirou and its castle, Lessay and its heath, Coutances and its cathedral, La Lucerne and its abbey. Real wonders of the Manche!

Swiss Normandy

Let's not exaggerate, even if they call it Swiss here, it is still in Normandy.

The traditions route

This is the region south of Caen where the bocage begins, with its hedgerows and meadows, before arriving at Vire with its famous andouille sausage. The traditions route is aimed at getting to know this undulating and attractive corner. Between Villers-Bocage, Dampierre and Caumont-l'Eventé, several little roads lead through charming landscapes. On the way you will find the forest which on the Jurques hills, has a zoological park.

Lace from Normandy

Seven towns have formed an association to organise the Normandy lace route. It bears witness to the skills of artisans with a very long and very beautiful history. Normandy is the only region in France reuniting the three techniques of the needle, the bobbin and filet lace. The lace makers taught their skills to the Venetians. They must have been really gifted... The circuit passes through the lace centres of Alençon, Argentan, Bayeux, Courseulles, La Perrière, Villedieules-Poêles and Caen.

Argentelles manor,
Villebadin (Orne).

Alençon lace.
(Monique Sclaresky collection)

INFORMATION – TOURIST ROUTES

- *Comité Régional de Tourisme (Evreux) : 02 32 33 79 00.*
- *Comité du Tourisme de Seine-Maritime (Bihorel-les-Rouen) : 02 35 59 26 26.*
- *Comité du Tourisme de l'Eure (Evreux) : 02 32 31 51 51.*
- *Comité du Tourisme du Calvados (Caen) : 02 31 86 53 30.*
- *Comité du Tourisme de la Manche (Saint-Lô) : 02 33 05 98 70.*
- *Comité du Tourisme de l'Orne (Alençon) : 02 33 28 88 71.*

PHOTOGRAVURE : NORD COMPO, VILLENEUVE-D'ASCQ (59)
© 2000 - ÉDILARGE SA, ÉDITIONS OUEST-FRANCE, RENNES
CET OUVRAGE A ÉTÉ ACHEVÉ D'IMPRIMER PAR L'IMPRIMERIE POLLINA À LUÇON (85) N° L80837
I.S.B.N. 2.7373.2693.1 - N° D'ÉDITEUR : 4072.01.06.06.00
DÉPÔT LÉGAL : JUIN 2000